SUSTAINING THE EARTH

Written by

Tim Cooper

Edited and designed by

David Muir

Cartoons by
Taffy

Published by **St John's Extension Studies**
Bramcote, Nottingham NG9 3RL

ISBN 1-900920-03-4

Printed in Great Britain by RPM Reprographics Ltd, Chichester.

St John's Extension Studies gratefully acknowledges permission from the following publishers to quote from their publications:

Bear and Company: for quotation from Claude Stewart *Cry of the Environment,* on page 5
Basil Blackwell: for quotations from Jonathon Porritt *Seeing Green* on pages 6, 53, 54
Cambridge University Press: for quotation from Donald Worster *Nature's Economy*, on page 19
Wm B Eerdmans Publishing Co: for quotations from Wesley Granberg-Michaelson *Tending the Garden*, on pages 7, 28; and for quotation from Albert Wolters *Creation Regained,* on page 35
HarperCollins: for quotations from Fritjof Capra *The Turning Point*, on pages 79, 83; for quotations from Porritt and Winner *The Coming of the Greens*, on pages 55, 59; and for quotations from Wesley Granberg-Michaelson *A Worldly Spirituality*, on pages 43, 110
Hodder and Stoughton: for quotations from James Houston *I Believe in the Creator*, on pages 27, 36
Inter-Varsity Press (USA): for quotations from Walsh and Middleton *The Transforming Vision*, on page 5
Marshall Pickering: for quotation from Steve Shaw *No Splits*, on page 63
Mowbrays/Cassell: for quotations from Kalliston Ware *The Orthodox Way*, on pages 25, 26, 27, 29, 33, 65
Penguin Books: for quotations from Keith Thomas *Man and the Natural World*, on page 18; and *Religion and the Decline of Magic*, on page 80
SCM Press: for quotations from Jürgen Moltmann *God in Creation,* on pages 25, 41, 63
Sphere Books: for quotations from E F Schumacher *Small is Beautiful*, on pages 50, 53, 55, 90
SPCK: for quotation from John Polkinghorne *Science and Providence*, on page 79
World Council of Churches: for quotations from Lesslie Newbiggin *The Other Side of 1984*, on pages 20-21; and from Thomas Sieger Derr *Ecology and Human Liberation*, on page 30

The **World Wide Fund for Nature UK** has supported the writing of this course.

CONTENTS

WHO THIS BOOK IS FOR

This workbook has been created to help all those who wish to examine a Christian view of the environment.

It may surprise many Christians to know that Christianity has a poor reputation when it comes to caring for the environment. It is not just that the *Church* is seen to have failed - it is also that Christian theology has often given a low priority to the sustenance of the created order. Some other religions, by making a closer link between the Creator and the created, have encouraged their adherents to regard the Earth as sacred.

It is our hope that some who do not hold Christian beliefs themselves, will find in this book an exposition (and where necessary, a defence) of Christian values in relation to creation, without, we hope, being unduly defensive about the track record of the Church.

But no doubt the majority of those who use this workbook will be Christians - Christians who wish to review their commitment to sustaining the created order, but wish to do it on an explicitly Christian basis. There are indeed strong Christian arguments for a careful attitude to creation, but in Christianity these are seen alongside other commitments - in particular to the renewal of the pinnacle of God's creation, the human species. This is not an easy task and the issues are complex. But we will fail to relate the Christian message to the concerns of our day if we do not make its ecological concerns clear. This is both an act of Christian integrity and an act of Christian proclamation, demonstrating that Christians are not merely following on behind secular environmental trends.

Why don't more Christians take such concerns more seriously? In an age when many already see the Church as out of step with their day-to-day lives, some Christians may hesitate to set the Church against the current consumer trend and isolate it yet further.

But perhaps more often it is simply because it is going to hurt. In the Western world we are locked into a consumer culture which functions on the abuse of the environment. It is painful to stand out against it. It will change the way we live, and life will not always be so convenient. With the pressures that many people live and work under already, this attitude is understandable. That is why we have created not just a workbook, but also a course of study with support from others. Realistically we are not likely to change without the discipline of revealing our thoughts to others for scrutiny, and without personal support from others who have been on this road before us.

This workbook is for those who want to think - and act - more Christianly in relation to the environment.

HOW TO USE THIS BOOK

This workbook can be used on several levels:

- It is designed in an open and "transparent" way so that you can find your way around it easily. You can therefore dip into it from time to time for information and insight.
- You can work through the workbook systematically, with or without using the ideas for further reading and study at the end of each Unit.
- You can do it alone, or form a group to discuss the issues raised.
- You can use it as the basis for a short course within the local church on environmental concerns.
- You can commit yourself to studying the issues contained the course, and submit written reflections on your work to a tutor. If you register for tutorial support (see the registration form at the end of the workbook), you will be sent further information on how to go about this and what work to submit.

We recommend the last option if you are serious about changing your own lifestyle in response to your studies. Few of us can do this without support, and if we are going to change our lives, it is particularly important that the Christian thinking that underlies the changes is solid.

SUSTAINING THE EARTH

UNIT 1

WORN OUT WORLD

CONTENTS

PURPOSE

The purpose of this Unit is to describe the impact of the human species on the rest of the natural environment, and to introduce some key ecological concepts.

THE DOMINANT SPECIES

All around us there is evidence of the impact which humankind has on the environment – buildings, fields, parks, quarries, roads, railways, canals. These all bear witness to our history of shaping the environment to meet *our* needs.

The human being is the most dominant species on Earth. And ever-greater knowledge and technological ingenuity is increasing our potential to alter the environment. Consider nuclear power and genetic engineering.

Industrial development has brought many benefits. The quality of housing is far better than in the past. We no longer need to import as much food as we did earlier this century. Electrical products have reduced the need for tiring physical work. And in general, people in the industrialised world are more mobile than ever before.

But these benefits must be offset against damage caused to the natural environment. In consuming more, the quality of air, land, rivers and seas has been sacrificed, and non-renewable supplies of energy and other resources are being depleted.

Wise care of the environment has not been integrated into our economic system. There is a profligate use of finite resources, considerable waste (not least in over-packaging), the deliberate artificial stimulation of "needs" through advertising, a tendency towards large-scale production and thus long distribution chains, and the use of many toxic substances with unknown health implications.

THE FEELBAD FACTOR

Despite the increase in affluence, many people sense that their quality of life has declined. We consume more, but do not necessarily feel any better. The countryside is scarred with roads and electricity pylons. Pollution of rivers and the sea makes bathing dangerous. The car poisons the air of urban areas, resulting in more and more children suffering from asthma.

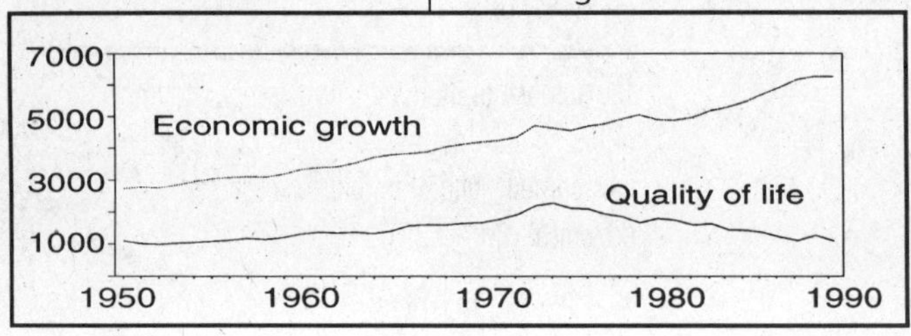

One of the most important international reports of recent years has been the Brundtland Commission's *Our Common Future*. This warned in 1987 that industrial development posed a major threat to the global environment. It called for *sustainable development*, defined as "development that meets the needs of the present without compromising the ability of future generations to meet their own needs."

Hands off?

Change to the natural environment over time is inevitable, but it is possible for us to live in harmony with our surroundings. Change need not necessarily be damaging.

In the midst of change, there is a need for preservation, keeping at least some land untouched by human activity. In Britain, however, even the wildest places have been affected by human activity during the course of history. There is little, if any, true "wilderness". As leisure has increased, isolated areas have become popular places for tourists, and consequently require careful environmental management to avoid erosion damage from walkers and other problems.

What we need is not a total "hands off" approach, but simply to ensure that future generations are left the same stock of "environmental assets" as we inherited – the same degree of fertility, biological diversity and so forth. And for this we need stronger will power and commitment.

Upsetting the balance

In the absence of due care, human activity leads to ecological instability and disruption to the "balance of nature".

Some examples will highlight the threat:

☛ We can destroy habitats at a local level by, for example, draining a small isolated area of wetland to improve agricultural potential. On the other hand, new habitats are also created through human developments such as canals, reservoirs, and railway verges.

☛ Habitat destruction can also take place at a global level. Climate change, caused by the emission of greenhouse gases, will affect habitats in many parts of the world.

☛ New species have been introduced, both intentionally (e.g. sycamore trees, grey squirrels) and as a result of accidental release from captivity (e.g. coypu, mink).

☛ People have made attempts to wipe out species, as in the 1950s when myxomatosis was deliberately spread to rabbits in an attempt to reduce damage to crops. Following the reduction in the number of rabbits, the wheatear, a ground nesting bird, suffered as a result of the disappearance of patches of heavily grazed grass (which had provided feeding areas) and the reduced number of burrows (which they used as nesting sites). And stoats, which eat rabbits, not surprisingly decreased in number. This example reveals the importance of appreciating the *interrelationships* in nature.

It is vital to acknowledge that we *choose* our impact on the natural environment.

In agriculture, for example, we maximise the productivity of desirable species such as wheat and thus inevitably reduce diversity. Consequently agriculture (in whatever form) is inherently unstable and can be maintained only with a high input of energy (e.g. weeding and harrowing) and materials (e.g. compost or fertiliser).

The increased environmental concern which *Our Common Future* stimulated led directly to the Rio Earth Summit in 1992. This set out a global programme, Agenda 21, for environmental sustainability.

THINK!

Serious environmental problems have been evident to many scientists for over thirty years, and yet "green" concerns have gained wide scale publicity only relatively recently. What do you think caused the delay?

There is one other alternative. In America a small group operates calling itself the voluntary human extinction movement. Its prospects for growth, however, do not appear promising.

HOW WE VIEW NATURE

Basic facts about global environmental problems are well known. The depletion of non-renewable resources, for example, is well documented.

Even at current consumption rates the number of years' supply of many basic commodities is disturbingly low.

In the table below the 2030AD consumption rate is based on 10bn people consuming at current US rates. "Reserves" means the quantities that can profitably be extracted with current technology; and "resources" means the total quantities thought to exist. (Source: Robert A Frosch and Nicholas E Gallopoulos, in *Scientific American*)

REMAINING GLOBAL RESOURCES
(in years)

	With current consumption		With 2030AD consumption	
	Reserves	*Resources*	*Reserves*	*Resources*
Aluminium	256	805	124	407
Coal	206	3,226	29	457
Cobalt	109	429	10	40
Copper	41	277	4	26
Molybdenum	67	256	8	33
Nickel	66	163	7	16
Platinum Group	225	413	21	29

Few deny that these are serious concerns. There is less agreement, however, concerning the exact nature of the crisis. Is it essentially political, economic, or technological? Where do the roots of the crisis lie?

Roots

The use of language can be revealing. An "environmental crisis" may imply that nature is fragile, not resilient enough to the pressures imposed by humankind. The problem is then seen as essentially *managerial* in character. It is thus to be solved by measures like more stringent environmental legislation or by taxes on energy and raw materials.

But the problems go beyond mere managerial failings. They are tied up with our relationship with our surroundings. There is a multitude of interrelated environmental crises, but the essential problem is an inner human crisis. Solutions require a profound shift in people's feelings and attitudes towards the environment.

How we perceive the world around us determines how we treat it.

GLOBAL CONCERNS

- 25,000 plant species and more than 1,000 vertebrate species and subspecies are threatened with extinction
- hundreds of millions of rural people in poor nations are compelled to destroy basic natural resources around them (such as trees and soil) to secure their short term survival
- 628 million people are threatened by desertification, of which 78 million are already affected by lower land productivity
- tropical rain forests are being felled or burned at a rate which would lead to their total disappearance after 85 years.
- every day 140 plant and animal species become extinct
- Six of the seven warmest years on record have occurred since 1980

Starting points

What determines the way in which we view our surroundings?

Each of us has a "world view", a set of assumptions we make about the basic make-up of the world. According to Brian Walsh and Richard Middleton, our world view "helps us interpret the world around us. It sorts out what is important from what is not, what is of highest value from what is least" (*The Transforming Vision)*.

Each person views the environment from a different perspective. A scientist may view nature as a collection of mechanically operating interconnected particles. An industrialist, on the other hand, may see it primarily as a stockpile of potential raw materials.

Metaphors can help us to articulate these basic perceptions and valuations. Claude Stewart has defined three metaphors of how we view our surroundings:

- nature is a machine which runs by itself
- nature is raw material or resource for human manipulation and consumption
- nature is the stage or scenery for the drama of human history

Stewart argues that these images are wholly at odds with a Biblical view. They imply that God is "pushed back from or excluded from nature in such a way and to such an extent as to make it very difficult to make sense out of claims that God acts in the world of nature." They have "tended to encourage the understanding of God as remote, insensitive, non-responsive, and incapable of being present in, or of effectively expressing the divine intentions through, nature" (*Cry of the Environment*). He suggests that instead we need metaphors which point to the integrity of nature. Sallie McFague, another theologian, proposes that we view the world as "God's body" (*Models of God*).

Nature has been described as having value of three types:

- instrumental value, in that it is useful to humankind
- instructional value, in that it may convey a sense of the presence of God
- intrinsic value, worth in itself irrespective of any benefits to humankind

If we value nature only for its usefulness to human beings we do not value it highly enough. Our view of nature is distorted.

Make a list of Biblical texts which suggest that nature has:

- instrumental value
- instructional value
- intrinsic value

Explain in each case how and why such value is often disregarded in modern society.

THINK!

Which metaphors do you identify with most closely in the discussion on this page? Has your image of nature changed over time?

A SPIRITUAL CRISIS

Many observers have argued that the ecological crisis has a fundamentally spiritual character and that ecology has implications for religious enquiry. They believe that the causes of environmental problems can only be understood with reference to the core beliefs about life which underpin human behaviour.

Ecology seeks to understand the *processes* which occur within nature, not simply its structure. It is a short step to ask about purpose. *Why* do these processes in nature take place?

Throughout history theologians, scientists and philosophers have sought an explanation for the natural order – the fact that nature operates consistently according to ecological principles. Early ecologists wrote of a desire to "find the hand of God in nature."

Contemporary writers and campaigners often write that what is needed is a new awareness of the world around us, a greater "consciousness" of our links with nature. We need to be life-centred (biocentric) rather than human-centred (anthropocentric).

"Some kind of spiritual commitment, or religion in its true meaning (namely, the reconnection between each of us and the source of all life), is a fundamental part of the transformation that ecologists are talking about."
Jonathon Porritt, *Seeing Green*

Beyond materialism

E.F. Schumacher, author of *Small is Beautiful*, described this need to think differently about the world around us, as "metaphysical reconstruction".

Such a change may take place for a number of reasons. It may be inspired by increased understanding of environmental science, a greater sense of the existence of a Creator, or a heightened concern about the future. Whatever the causes, people begin to see the world around them in a new light and develop their environmental awareness at a deeper level.

Many environmentalists believe that the degradation of the natural world is the result of a crisis which is essentially spiritual. Although many are not Christians, they would accept that there is another dimension to life beyond the material.

This dimension is that which inspires our innermost thoughts and feelings. It is the source of our sense of awe at the natural world, the basis for our moral choices, and the driving force behind our behaviour.

Life with purpose?

As humans we are inextricably bound to the structure of nature. How do we understand our place within the natural order? Are we merely collections of atoms, bundles of cells, brought together through evolution and subject to nature's cycles ("ashes to ashes, dust to dust"). Is there any fundamental difference between humans and other species?

And we are also part of the functioning of nature. How do we understand our role in the working of the natural world? Do humans serve any special function or purpose within the natural order?

Christianity teaches that humans are indeed qualitatively distinct from other life-forms, being created in the image of God. At the same time, "a person exists only in relation" (Paulos Gregorios). We are apart from nature, but also a part of nature.

Look up the following Bible texts: Gen 2:7, Gen 2:15, Ps 24:1. Try to write down three things the Bible seems to tell us about our human relationship with the Earth. Then look in the margin of page 9 for some comments.

A poor track record

Adherents of the world's major faiths have not always set the best example for environmental care. Christianity in particular has sometimes taught negative attitudes to the environment. We will consider this in more detail in the next Unit.

"Western Christianity has been quick to stress humanity's role to 'rule over and subdue' the earth ... [but the Bible] makes more sense when we realise that it is a story of how God, humanity, and the creation relate to each other."

Granberg-Michaelson, *Tending the Garden*

THE POOP TEST?

Some years ago, reformed theologian Eugene Heideman wrote a perceptive and original article highlighting the goodness of biological life in God's eyes (in *Third Way*, February 1986).

He argued that biological existence is a time of blessing in spite of all its limitations. Even at the outset of creation it appears that species died. Otherwise Adam would have had no concept of death when warned about the consequence of eating from the tree of knowledge.

Through the incarnation of Jesus, God reaffirmed the goodness of biological existence. Jesus experienced life in an ordinary human body prior to the resurrection, with all its pleasures and limitations. Like Him, our resurrection body will be very different from the biological bodies which we now have (1 Cor 15:35-50).

Heideman concluded his article with a novel test of how "good" we really believe it is that God created a biological world:

"Our attitude toward manure can serve as a gauge of how 'good' we believe it is that God created a biological world. It is easy enough to thank him for a glorious sunset or the marvellous flavour of an apple. But our gratitude develops

a new dimension when in the midst of our technology and our economic systems we can sincerely thank him even for the excrement that feeds the trees, the flowers, the grass."

Heideman proposed that "if we take the biological dimension of creation seriously we will recognise that death is simply the sign of the finitude of all created beings rather than some ultimate tragedy of evil."

Do you agree with him? What are the implications of such a view for our use of other species?

WHAT IS ECOLOGY?

According to leading scholar Eugene Odum ecology is "the study of the structure and function of nature".

The roots of the term ecology are the Greek words *oikos* meaning house or place to live, and *logos* meaning discourse or study.

The Chambers Dictionary defines ecology as the "study of plants, or of animals, or of peoples and institutions, in relation to environment".

The term ecology was coined by the German biologist Ernst Haeckel in the late 1860s to mean "the science of the relations of living organisms to the living world".

Ecology focuses on the interconnections between different life forms. This raises issues concerning how life is sustained and the future prospects for life on our planet. It is a vitally important subject, but one which, regrettably, relatively few people study.

Is ecology a science?

Most academic ecologists hold that it is. Some regard it as a branch of biology.

Others disagree, as we will see in Unit 5. They point out that nature can be studied in many ways, not just using scientific methodologies. The Romantic poets, the American "transcendentalists" and the contemporary "deep ecology" movement are equally part of the ecology tradition. Some people may understand nature through "objective" experimentation and analysis but others find that they learn as much through the direct experience of living in close proximity with nature.

What is the source of this tension? Walsh and Middleton have traced a division between sciences and humanities to the 19th century, when scholars feared that determinism in scientific study might encroach into other subjects. Science was supposed to explain natural reality in terms of strictly lawful relations of cause and effect, while the humanities considered human reality in terms of people's choices.

From a Christian perspective such a strict division is questionable. As God is sovereign, scientific laws are no more than provisional theoretical approximations of how He orders creation. Although God's laws are universal – which explains the order in nature – there is also a degree of freedom which is bound up with the human response to God. Creation contains both uniqueness and individuality.

Are there inevitable conflicts between scientific and religious methodologies? Do concepts such as the sovereignty and authority of God help or hinder your understanding of the natural environment? Why?

Principles of ecology

There are certain widely accepted ecological principles or laws. These explain why the biosphere tends to display consistent behaviour.

- **All species are interdependent or interrelated.**

This is the most fundamental of the principles. Humankind is as integral to the global ecosystem as any other species and equally subject to its norms – although we are, to a unique extent, able to modify our environment.

- **The biosphere displays order.**

It is evident from observation that the processes of life do not follow a random pattern, but are generally consistent. At the same time there appear to be inexplicable exceptions. "Chaos theory" is the attempt to explore the unpredictable occurrences of, among other things, sudden climatic change.

- **Living systems tend towards a condition of balance.**

This balance constitutes a "steady-state" in which the system's components (it's organisms) are in harmony with each other. It is achieved by a process of self-regulation, in which the living organisms attempt to adjust themselves to changes in the availability of energy and materials. The biosphere may in its entirety be seen as a system, as in the Gaia hypothesis (see page 81).

- **The resources of the Earth are finite.**

The Earth contains a limited quantity of resources. There is no more carbon available today than when life first appeared. Once we have used all the oil and coal, there is no way (in the likely lifetime of the human species) that any more will be created for us.

ANSWERS

from page 7

Being created in God's image, we have a special role on Earth. We are here to love and serve God (Deut 6:5,13). We have a special capacity to respond to God and our relationship to the Earth is inextricably linked to our relationship with Him. Nature functions well, from a human perspective, when we act in accordance with His will (Deut 28:2,4 cf. Is 24:4,5).

We were made from the Earth (Gen 2:7). We are called to care for it (Gen 2:15), and we should remember that it is God who owns it (Ps 24:1). Ecology is important because if we understand the unfolding processes of life we will be better equipped to take care of the world.

INTERPRETING THE WORLD AROUND US

What then does ecology teach us about the structure and function of nature?

The Earth is a community

Ecology is concerned with the *biosphere*, that part of the Earth and its surrounding atmosphere where living things are found.

Any environment has both *biotic* (living) and *abiotic* (non-living) components. Defined areas within which communities of organisms live and function together are known as *ecosystems*.

The "systems approach" sees the Earth as dynamic and integrated. Organisms are studied interacting within their environment, and their working relationships are considered important. This contrasts with the practice of studying individual plants and animals in isolation.

A *population* is a group of organisms of the same species which occupies a particular place at a particular time. A group of animals and plants living together is a *community*. The total population of a species which the environment can support in a state of balance is its *carrying capacity*. This will be affected by factors which vary from year to year, such as rainfall.

Each organism has a particular part to play in the community, its *niche*. Over time, organisms may adapt to their environment, either behaviourally or structurally, in order to perform a role or fit a niche.

The Earth is always changing

In any living environment changes take place as organisms that are well-adapted become dominant; this is called *ecological succession*. An unused field, once bare, might in turn be covered with lichens and algae, then weeds and grasses, then small bushes and shrubs and, finally, large trees. Each definable stage in the process of change is a *sere* and when the system stabilises (becomes "mature") it is said to reach a *climax*.

Some ecosystems are more stable than others; as a general rule those that are *complex* (that is, include many organisms) tend to be most stable. There are exceptions, such as the Arctic. Pollution, disease, and natural disasters such as earthquakes, floods and volcano eruptions can bring instability.

The Earth is a web of relationships

In the biosphere, relationships between organisms are important. The food chain, for example, links them according to eating behaviour. A rose may be eaten by a greenfly, which in turn is eaten by a ladybird, which is eaten by a hedgehog. In any ecosystem there is normally a multitude of food chains, each interconnected. Collectively they are known as *food webs*.

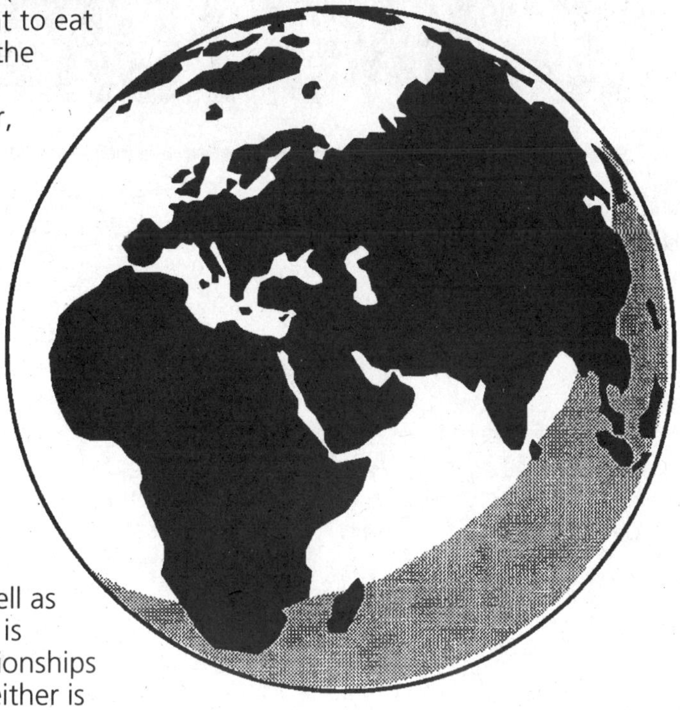

Where two organisms (whether plants or animals) want to eat the same food or use the same light, they are in *competition*. However, different species by definition tend to exploit different resources, thereby limiting competition. Competitive behaviour for resources and space is an important influence upon the population of species, especially where they occupy a similar niche.

But co-operation as well as competitive behaviour is evident. In some relationships between organisms neither is harmed and one helps another. An example of this is lichens, where the alga provides food by photosynthesising and the fungus provides support. This is known as *symbiosis*. Some creatures "groom" others by eating their parasites, while some are transported by others. Certain fish rely on other sea creatures for protection. Many plants require the co-operation of insects to achieve fertilization.

Another form of relationship is *parasitism*, where one organism lives in or on the other, the host, and derives food from it. A flea is an *ectoparasite*, living *on* the host, while a tapeworm is an *endoparasite*, living *in* the host.

The complex set of relationships between organisms in a community is known as a *species-network*.

The Earth works in cycles

Life processes on the Earth take place through cycles, such as the carbon cycle, nitrogen cycle and water cycle. Such natural "recycling" allows the limited supply of chemicals on Earth to be used continuously.

Thus when organisms die, scavengers and decomposers feed on the dead organic matter, and carbon dioxide and minerals are eventually released for reuse, enabling plants to grow. Human activity sometimes disrupts these cycles by moving materials or polluting them.

But...

The exception to these cyclical processes is energy. Energy flows through an ecosystem but is not recycled. Some is always being lost to the system as heat or in some other form. For life to continue, therefore, there has to be a continuous source of energy – the sun.

Our industrial activities are rapidly consuming energy in the form of coal, oil, and gas which has taken many thousands of years to be created. These fossil fuels are, in effect, stored solar energy from an earlier era.

GOING FURTHER

Our view of the world

Exploring the historical development of Christian attitudes to nature, theologian Paul Santmire (*The Travail of Nature*) identifies three helpful metaphors relating to our experience of the world. Two of them, the metaphor of ascent and the metaphor of fecundity, relate to what he terms "the experience of the overwhelming mountain".

On climbing a mountain, a person may seek to leave behind the "mundane" things of the Earth and, looking to the infinite reaches of the sky above, experience a sense of transcendence. Alternatively, that person may rise to a vantage point from which to look down and gain a new perspective of the Earth's vastness, mystery and beauty.

The former gives birth to *the metaphor of ascent,* which is essentially negative towards the Earth. Santmire sees this represented in the Bible most clearly in John's Gospel, which contains images of Christ descending to Earth in order that he might later ascend, carrying His followers upward with Him, leaving this world behind (John 6:44, 12:32).

In contrast, the latter perspective gives birth to *the metaphor of fecundity*, which is essentially positive towards the Earth. Santmire sees this represented in the Bible in the covenant made with all creatures (Gen 9:9-11), songs of praise to the Creator in numerous Psalms (e.g. Ps 104), and in the promise of the renewal of the whole creation (Is 11:6-9, Rom 8:18-21, Col 1:19-20).

His third metaphor is *the metaphor of migration to a good land*. This is portrayed in Deuteronomy in the story of the Israelites being led by Moses towards a "land of milk and honey". In that it is a promising journey in which the idea of "land" is never left behind, it is essentially positive towards nature.

Additional reading

For those who wish to deepen their knowledge of the scientific dimension, key texts include E.P. Odum's *Basic Ecology*, David Owen's *What is Ecology?* and Paul Ehrlich's *The Machinery of Nature.* From a more political perspective there is Jonathon Porritt's influential (but slightly dated) *Seeing Green* and Croall and Rankin's amusing *Ecology for Beginners*. Sam Berry, an evangelical and former President of the British Ecological Society, has written *God and the Biologist*, while Ghillean Prance, Director of the Royal Botanic Gardens, Kew, has produced *The Earth Under Threat: A Christian Perspective*.

For the very keen

Donald Worster, *Nature's Economy* (especially Chapters 1-5)
Donald Worster traces the history of ecology commencing in the eighteenth century. Summarise the contribution made by Gilbert White, Carl Linnaeus and Henry David Thoreau to our modern understanding of ecology and explain the tension which emerged between Romanticism and Christianity.

Sean McDonagh, *The Greening of the Church* (especially Chapters 1-3)
From his experience of life in the Philippines Father McDonagh addresses the impact of debt, population growth and deforestation on low income countries. What, in each case, are the religious and political obstacles that must be overcome if solutions to the problems are to be found?

SUSTAINING THE EARTH

UNIT 2

POINTING THE FINGER

CONTENTS

PURPOSE

The purpose of this Unit is to explore some of the reasons why environmental problems have arisen, including the impact of the Enlightenment and negative attitudes to nature within the Christian tradition.

A CASE TO ANSWER

If we are to improve the quality of the natural environment we first need to understand the reasons why things have gone wrong. It isn't enough simply to blame sin. Nor is it enough to point the finger at one or another political system. We need to probe further.

> ***Who or what is really to blame for our current misuse of the Earth?***

The case for the prosecution

As environmental awareness developed rapidly in the late 1960s and early 1970s, Christianity was forced on the defensive, accused of teaching negative attitudes to nature.

The most influential attack was a notorious speech in 1966 by an American historian, Professor Lynn White Jr., in which he called for the rejection of "the Christian axiom that nature has no reason for existence save to serve man." White's case may be summarised as follows:

❶ Modern science and technology are distinctively Western. Following the translation of Arabic and Greek scientific works into Latin in the 11th century, scientific leadership had, by the late 13th century, shifted from the Islamic world to Europe.

❷ Christianity established a dualism of humankind and nature. Insisting that God's will is for humankind to exploit nature "for his proper ends", it became "the most anthropocentric religion the world has ever seen."

❸ Western science and technology have grown out of Christian attitudes towards our relation to nature. The initial motivation for scientific enquiry was rooted in Christian belief.

❹ No new set of basic values has been accepted in Western society to displace those of Christianity. White concluded that Christianity was still highly influential.

"The victory of Christianity over paganism was the greatest psychic revolution in the history of our culture... By destroying pagan animism Christianity made it possible to exploit nature in a mood of indifference to the feelings of natural objects... The spirits in natural objects, which formerly had protected nature from man, evaporated."

Lynn White, "The Historic Roots of our Ecologic Crisis" in *Science* Vol 155 (1967)

The case for the defence

What was Christianity's defence? In response to White, the Archbishop of Canterbury, Dr. Michael Ramsey, set up a doctrinal working group to study the theological basis for attitudes to nature. Its report, *Man and Nature*, included a critique of White's article by Arthur Peacocke.

White's claim that Christianity caused the scientific revolution was challenged on two grounds: that science had emerged within *non*-Christian cultures, and that it did not flourish *throughout* Christendom. The case against White was as follows:

❶ Science arose without the benefit of Christianity in China, ancient Greece and medieval Islam.
Not all scholars would argue that Christianity paved the way for scientific progress. Beliefs associated with the rise of secular humanism may have been more significant.

❷ The Bible does not depict nature as existing only for the benefit of humankind.
Most Biblical scholars would reject simplified interpretations of human dominion in Genesis, which have given the impression that Christianity is inherently negative to nature.

❸ There is a divergence in attitudes to science and technology within the Judaeo-Christian tradition.
While technology flourished in the Christian culture of Western Europe, it did not in the East, even in Christian circles. Cultural temperament, as distinct from Christian doctrine, may account for different attitudes to technology.

❹ Exploitation of the natural environment has occurred from the earliest times and not just during the Judaeo-Christian era.
Almost every civilization, including Hindu and Buddhist cultures, has abused the environment by deforestation and overgrazing.

White himself recognised the cultural influences on Christianity. He pointed to historic differences between theological developments in the Eastern, Greek-speaking churches and Western, Latin churches.

Each of the steps in White's reasoning can be exposed as questionable. But however much White may have overstated the case, it would be wrong to suggest that Christianity does not shoulder some of the blame for environmental degradation.

In *The Travail of Nature* theologian Paul Santmire describes how, over many centuries, Christians have arrived at very different beliefs concerning nature. He identifies a *nature-affirming* tradition and a *nature-denying* tradition.

☛ In the **nature-affirming** tradition, the human spirit is understood as rooted in the world of nature. There is an instinctive desire among God's people to celebrate His presence in all things. Santmire sees Irenaeus, the "mature" Augustine, and (to a degree) Luther and Calvin as in this theological tradition.

☛ In the **nature-denying** tradition, nature is regarded as of no intrinsic worth and the world is not considered our "proper home". This view has perhaps been more dominant. Santmire sees it represented in the writings of Origen, Bonaventure, Dante, Barth and Teilhard de Chardin. It is worth considering in a little more depth.

In his 1966 lecture, Lynn White proposed St. Francis as a "patron saint for ecologists." Pope John Paul II made him a saint in 1979. Can you think of any modern-day ecological saints?

The Eastern churches were inclined to treat sin as intellectual blindness and considered that salvation was to be found in illumination, or "clear thinking". In contrast, the Western churches taught that sin was moral evil and that salvation was achieved through "right conduct". Hence White concluded: "The Greek saint contemplates; the Western saint acts. The implications of Christianity for the conquest of nature would emerge more easily in the Western atmosphere."

Another influential study in the 1970s was Thomas Sieger Derr's *Ecology and Human Liberation*.

THE CHURCH AGAINST NATURE?

Christians throughout history have held some negative attitudes to nature. None of them are integral to authentic Christian belief, but they need to be understood if they are to be countered.

Human-centred

In the West Christians have tended to treat the Bible as the story of God working in the world through human beings, as distinct from a history of the whole creation. It has been assumed that humankind is at the centre of purpose and meaning in the universe. This is an "anthropocentric" world view.

It follows that the natural world has been created solely for our benefit. The result has been human pride, or *hubris*, and an undervaluation and exploitation of other species.

The Genesis story invites us to shape the world, to work the Earth. We are not called to be passive, to let the world "take its own course". At the same time, however, we are called to take care of the Earth (Gen 2:15).

A distant God

Many Christians have seen God as distant from the world and not interacting intimately with it. He is a *God of being* – distant, unchanging and unresponsive, rather than a *God of becoming* – close, active and responsive.

There have been good reasons for this. Christians have feared that too close an association of God with nature would revitalise paganism. Before the arrival of Christianity nature was seen as the home of numerous deities dwelling in or amidst particular species or places.

But this distancing of God from the Earth meant that people lost a sense of the sacred in nature. Ultimately nature was regarded as unworthy of our care because people no longer saw any divine expression within it.

The Biblical metaphors for God of *king* and *ruler* are "hierarchical, imperialistic and dualistic, stressing the distance between God and the world and the total reliance of the world on God" (Sallie McFague, *Models of God*). Alternative metaphors of *mother*, *lover* and *friend* are less evident in the Bible, but may be more appropriate to the concerns of our present age because they are associated with reciprocity, love and shared responsibility for the world.

Otherworldly

Christianity has often focused on the positive value of "life away from the world"– in the church or in heaven.

A popular evangelical chorus includes the lines: "This world is not my home; I'm just a-passing through."

One theologian has suggested that it is because human beings have a "non-natural dimension" distinguishing us from the rest of creation, that we are "never completely at home in the natural world" (Thomas Sieger Derr, *Ecology and Human Liberation*). Redemption is often interpreted not as a refinement or purification of the Earth but as a means of escape from it (cf. 1 Pet 3.10-13).

Santmire points out that such beliefs are based on a selective reading of particular passages in the Bible. Parts of John's gospel and the epistle to the Hebrews, for example, can suggest that the world is of little value and that we will in due course escape from it. But Paul's epistles to the Colossians and Ephesians convey a more positive understanding of our place in creation.

Political disengagement

Most Christians refrain from any active interest or participation in politics, believing that non-involvement represents political neutrality. In reality it represents a conservative stance, as it implicitly affirms the status quo.

Environmental issues have a political dimension. The human impact on the environment is influenced by the way in which we organise and govern ourselves. C.S. Lewis recognised this when he wrote: "What we call man's power over nature turns out to be a power exercised by some men over other men with nature as its instrument" (*The Abolition of Man*).

Those Christians who *are* politically involved tend to focus on social issues. Caring for the environment is seen as a distraction from caring for other *people* ("we can't do everything"). Even radical advocates of liberation theology have often failed to acknowledge that freedom from poverty demands environmentally-sustainable development, and are inclined to argue that God is discovered through a historical struggle rather than the natural revelation.

MAN OR NEWT

Who Needs a Home More?

Your church has decided to take a greater interest in local concerns. One local pressure group has written to you asking church members to campaign to prevent a housing development which will threaten the site of a rare species of newt, while another group has written on behalf of the homeless.

What criteria do you use in determining which group to support? Or do you reply to each of them by saying that the church should not get involved in local politics?

Three questions

Here are three questions, the answers to which will reveal a Christian's attitude to nature:

Q1 Does the Bible grant human beings unqualified dominion over His creation? (Gen 1:28, Gen 2:15)

Q2 Is the spiritual world distinct and separate from the material world? (1 Cor 15:53, Jam 2:15-16)

Q3 Is the Earth to be destroyed at the end of time? (2 Pet 3:10, Col 1:19-20)

"Most modern Western theology assumes that the relationship of God to *human* experience, either personally or historically, is the centre of the theological task." (Wesley Granberg-Michaelson, in "Why Christians Lost an Environmental Ethic")

Does this satisfactorily explain why nature has been devalued in the Christian church? What would *you* consider to be the central task of theology?

THINK!

What are the practical implications for *you* of believing that our destiny lies beyond the normal confines of space (the known universe) and time (Earthly history)?

OTHER CULPRITS

"Culture" comprises the customs, ideas, values, technical processes, and social organisation, which human beings superimpose on the sphere of nature. Christianity has certainly helped to shape the Western culture which has so abused the Earth in recent years. But there have been other influences. Many of these were part of the Enlightenment, the ideas of the period immediately prior to the scientific advances which led to industrialisation. These too were important in promoting the exploitation of nature. They include:

Dualism and Mechanism

The assumption of dualism is that the world is divided into two contrasting elements which are separate and fundamentally different (see page 65). In particular, mind is contrasted with matter and spirit is contrasted with bodies. Such thinking is also extended to other areas:

☛ one area of life is viewed as sacred and another as secular
☛ work and leisure are compartmentalised
☛ men and women are regarded as entirely different

"Descartes's explicit aim had been to make men 'lord and possessors of nature'. It fitted in well with his intention that he should have portrayed other species as inert and lacking any spiritual dimension. In so doing he created an absolute break between man and the rest of nature, thus clearing the way very satisfactorily for the uninhibited exercise of human rule."
Keith Thomas, *Man and the Natural World*

The key source of modern dualism is the 17th century deist philosopher Rene Descartes, although it is a tradition which can be traced back to Plato. Descartes argued that our capacity to *think* is the one aspect of reality which cannot be doubted: hence his celebrated claim *Cogito ergo sum* – "I think, therefore I am." As human beings alone have the capacity for rational thought (and thus a soul), Descartes concluded that we are fundamentally different from the rest of nature.

Moreover, according to this world view the material universe operates essentially like a machine. Everything in the material world is explained in terms of the arrangement and movement of its parts. Matter is considered to have no purpose, life or spirituality of its own.

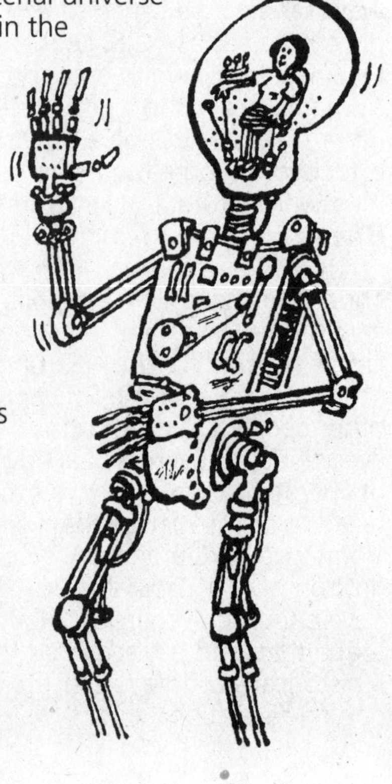

Thus nature (even the human body) is seen as working according to mechanical laws. According to Descartes animals could be regarded as mere machines. Before long they were treated as such in experiments.

The logic of dualism is that the material world is denigrated. This has two possible outcomes:

☛ In the ascetic tradition the material world is thought of as a threat to spiritual life and people *withdraw* from worldly activity.

☛ The dominant response, however, has been that nature is no longer treated as sacred or having intrinsic value and is consequently *exploited*.

Reductionism and Individualism

In the search for scientific knowledge about the natural world, organisms were often studied as if self-contained and self-sufficient. The methodology was a simplifying process involving breaking up complex systems into parts – a form of reductionism.

The primary objection to reductionism is that it effectively denies the significance of relationships. In scientific ecology relationships are normally regarded as crucial (although there is a branch of study called "autecology" in which individual organisms are studied). Reductionism thus contrasts with the methodology normally associated with ecology (see page 64).

> ***"Breaking nature down into its atomistic parts cannot result in a true understanding of the whole. Special qualities emerge out of interactions and collectivities: the whole of nature is different from the sum of its parts."***
> **Donald Worster, *Nature's Economy***

A key feature of Enlightenment thought was the importance attached to the autonomy of individuals. "There is no such thing as society" Margaret Thatcher once declared. Such beliefs are still prevalent. The value of the individual is emphasised, and is defended against the kind of collectivism which crushes personal initiative.

But leading environmental campaigner Jonathon Porritt warns of the "curse of individualism" because it not only conflicts with biological support systems but creates needless conflict and exacerbates loneliness and alienation.

Materialism

By denigrating the material world and denying that nature is in any sense sacred, dualism enabled the development of materialism. Since the start of the industrial era, progress has been measured by the amount of wealth consumed. The acquisition of material goods has increasingly been regarded as the only source of meaning and purpose.

The natural environment is exploited because it is not valued highly in economic terms.

Attempts have in fact been made to quantify the value of the environment. Many economists argue that the price of goods should reflect the full cost to the environment of their production, including cleaning up any pollution. There are, however, problems in identifying prices for "environmental assets" which are not traded in any market, such as clean air or the existence of a particular species.

Some critics also question how aesthetic and intrinsic value can be taken into account, as this cannot readily be translated into monetary units. They argue that attempts at valuing nature are fundamentally flawed as they reinforce the assumption that only those things which can be quantified are important.

ACCEPTING RESPONSIBILITY

It is not easy to identify the religious and cultural factors which have been most influential in determining our negative attitudes to nature. Our perception of nature, the value we attach to it and how we use it are determined by variety of religious and cultural influences. These often depend upon and reinforce each other.

The extent to which people are religious (or, more specifically, Christian) may help to shape a nation's culture, while at the same time the cultural context within which they live may affect their religious beliefs.

Christianity and culture

The classic text for understanding how Christianity relates to culture is Richard Niebuhr's *Christ and Culture*. Niebuhr identifies several different approaches, of which the two extremes are:

Christ against culture
Christian thought and action are diametrically opposed. Christianity is about preaching and prophecy, not art, philosophy or politics. Such a tendency is seen in the Plymouth Brethren and in the Amish community in Pennsylvania, USA.

The Christ of culture
Christianity is associated with existing cultural views and programmes for action. This is especially evident in political movements where people directly equate their Christian beliefs with their political activities as with liberation theology, Christian Socialism and America's Moral Majority movement.

No new values?

Lynn White claimed that no new set of basic values had displaced those of Christianity. Even twenty years ago, however, most evangelicals and many liberals would have denied that a Christian world view was dominant in the West. A more credible case for cultural dominance could be made for secular humanism.

There is an important tradition of Christian opposition to industrialism, which is documented in Martin Weiner's *English Culture and The Decline of the Industrial Spirit.*

New ideas and values emerged during the Enlightenment, including belief in the progress and the perfectibility of "man". These led to a human arrogance which certainly had a profound effect on people's relationship with the natural environment.

According to Lesslie Newbigin people today put more faith in contemporary science than religious beliefs. "The modern scientific world view is taught as a true account of how things are, while religion is taught as an aspect of culture which is available in a variety of styles" (*The Other Side of 1984*).

Other social commentators, notably eco-feminists, point to the significance of patriarchy (male dominance) in the industrialised West. They draw parallels between the male exploitation of women and of nature.

In short, there are a great many factors apart from Christianity, which have affected our use of the environment.

Reversing the trend

But Christianity has not been blameless. Christians often fit well into contemporary Western culture. "Why doesn't the word Christian conjure up images of people turning the world upside down?" ask Brian Walsh and Richard Middleton in *The Transforming Vision*.

As Christians we tend to be reactive rather than pro-active. We respond to change rather than leading it. "The attempts by Christians to formulate a Christian environmental ethic are for the most part following, not setting, a general cultural trend", writes Loren Wilkinson in *Tending the Garden*. Yet there are, belatedly, signs that the church is responding to environmental concern, with a new wave of Christian environmental initiatives, books and events.

"Christian faith in the West has been captive to the assumptions of modern culture which sever God from creation and subject the creation to humanity's arrogant and unrestrained power. Unlike Lynn White, I believe our problem lies in the church's historical captivity to Western culture rather than the reverse."

Wesley Granberg-Michaelson, "Why Christians Lost an Environmental Ethic"

Some theologians have suggested that Western Christians should turn to Eastern Orthodoxy for help in developing a more nature-affirming theology. Eastern Orthodoxy lacks the individualistic emphasis of Western Christianity. All of nature is seen as sacred, and redemption is understood as God acting in Jesus Christ to reconcile the whole cosmos to Himself.

Would you agree that Western culture has been so powerfully moulded by Christianity that the basic values in the West remain Christian? Has Christianity had so great an impact that it can be regarded as the primary cause of environmental degradation? Write your thoughts down here.

ST PAUL AND CULTURE

In the early church, the apostle Paul's Christian teaching conflicted with contemporary Greek culture, with its dualistic philosophy. The Greeks despised the necessity of manual work, and sought to be free from it in order to pursue recreation, politics, philosophy or religion. Paul however did not regard religion as a "spiritual" activity, separate from work.

GOING FURTHER

Disgracing the world

How has dualism, which separates the material from spiritual, influenced Christian thought? One example is in relation to nature and grace.

In the medieval era Thomas Aquinas argued that the effects of God's grace permeate the whole realm of nature, not just human beings. In this sense he was positive towards nature and acknowledged the goodness of all creation.

Aquinas did not, however, regard nature on the same level as grace. He believed that nature existed to serve God's grace. Thus nature is, in effect, reduced to a mere *instrument* of the "supernatural" gift of grace.

Claude Stewart has described the triumph of images of nature as machine, resource and stage (see page 5) as resulting in a "dis-gracing" of nature. It denies the operation of God's grace in nature.

Reformed theologians Walsh, Middleton and Wolters conclude that the theology of Aquinas needs to be turned on its head. The purpose of grace, they argue, is to restore nature (see Albert M. Wolters, *Creation Regained* and Walsh and Middleton, *The Transforming Vision*).

Additional reading

Lynn White Jr.'s lecture was reproduced in the journal *Science* (Vol. 155, No. 3767, 10th March 1967). One of the most influential recent critiques of Western culture and modern science is Fritjof Capra's *The Turning Point*. The historic emergence of ecology is described in Donald Worster's *Nature's Economy*. Keith Thomas's excellent *Man and the Natural World* describes the important changes in attitudes which took place between the 16th and 19th century. Wesley Granberg-Michaelson's article "Why Christianity Lost an Environmental Ethic" (*Epiphany*, Winter 1988) is a useful summary from a Christian perspective. Andrew Linzey and Tom Regan have edited a useful reader, *Animals and Christianity*, containing extracts from key theologians on the animal creation.

For the very keen

Ian Bradley, *God is Green*
Ian Bradley sets out his claim that Christianity's "green" credentials have been distorted by alien influences and human selfishness. Comparing his interpretation of history and scripture with that of Lynn White, explain why they arrive at contrasting conclusions.

Keith Thomas, *Man and the Natural World*, Chapters 1, 3 & 4
In this study of English attitudes to the natural world Professor Thomas describes how people's closer affinity with animals gradually weakened assumptions about human uniqueness. How important a factor was Christianity in the subsequent "dethronement of man"?

H. Paul Santmire, *The Travail of Nature*, Chapters 1, 2, 9 & 10
A systematic and historical study of theologians' attitudes to nature. In the light of the state of the global environment, do you expect the ecological motif to triumph over the spiritual motif in theological debate? How persuasive do you find the spiritual motif?

SUSTAINING THE EARTH

UNIT 3

WHERE IN THE WORLD IS GOD?

CONTENTS

PURPOSE

The purpose of this Unit is to further our understanding of how God works in and through His creation and how our experience of nature may deepen our awareness of the presence of God.

TOO CLOSE FOR COMFORT

Much of the material in this unit is taken from chapter 5 of Tim Cooper's *Green Christianity*.

People in the industrialised West may understand more about nature in scientific terms than previous generations, but many of us have lost our sense of how God works through nature.

- How we understand God affects how we perceive the environment.
- Our understanding of God also determines our answer to the question: "How is the natural order sustained?"

Christians in the West tend to assume that God acts in His creation entirely through human beings, and essentially through their minds and spirits. This is seen as God's chosen "way in" to the world He once created. Since He works through *willing* minds and spirits, He works essentially through Christians or the Church. When He intervenes in the "natural world", perhaps in response to our prayers, we call it a miracle.

As we will see, this is a questionable way of looking at the world. God is continually active in the natural world. If there is an unusual change in nature, it may be that God is doing something new.

But our way of looking at things is understandable, given our past.

Our pagan past

The modern Christian view of God contrasts with *pagan and animist* beliefs, which locate God in nature.

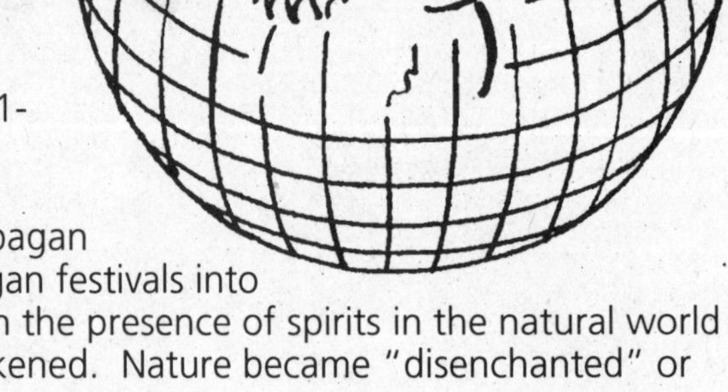

For a long period in history the main challenge to Christianity was paganism and animism. The Church justified its opposition to such beliefs by pointing to Biblical injunctions differentiating the Divine from the natural world (e.g. Exod 20:4, Deut 4:15-40, 7:5, 12:2-4, Jer 10:1-11).

Sometimes the Church absorbed pagan rituals, for example by turning pagan festivals into Christian ones. Gradually, belief in the presence of spirits in the natural world – in trees, wells and stones – weakened. Nature became "disenchanted" or "desacralised".

A distant God?

Another challenge to mainstream Christianity has been a belief that God created the world but is separate from it, distant and uninvolved. God is pushed away from the Earth and up into the heavens. This belief, called *deism*, became common after the Enlightenment, although its origins can be traced to the Neo-Platonism of Greek philosophy.

Some Christians today believe that God is incapable of emotion (*impassible*) and incapable of change (*immutable*). This wholly transcendent God, influenced by deism, lacks any real interaction with the world.

Pan-en-theism

Martin Luther wrote that although God fills the world He is not encompassed and surrounded by it.

Pantheism, the belief that the material world is the living expression of the essence of God, is rejected by Christians. The Christian doctrine of creation brings God and nature into relation, but also distinguishes them.

But *panentheism*, the belief that God is in all things and everything is in God, is accepted by a growing number of Christians. Panentheism emphasises the interaction between God and His creation. "God is always at the heart of each thing, maintaining it in being" (Kallistos Ware, *The Orthodox Way*).

Panentheism thus differs in a subtle but crucial way from pantheism. "Whereas simple pantheism makes everything a matter of indifference, panentheism is capable of differentiation. Whereas simple pantheism sees merely eternal, divine presence, panentheism is able to discern future transcendence, evolution and intentionality" (Jurgen Moltmann, *God in Creation*).

In his doctrine of "creation in the Spirit", Moltmann describes creation as a dynamic web of interconnected processes. The Creator Spirit, who indwells creation, differentiates and yet binds together, preserves and yet leads living things and their communities beyond themselves.

"God is substantially present everywhere, in and through all creatures, in all their parts and places, so that the world is full of God and He fills all, but without His being encompassed and surrounded by it. He is at the same time outside and above all creatures."

Martin Luther

Which of these three views of God's relationship to creation (paganism, deism and panentheism) do you think best reflects what you read in the Bible? Is there a *better* way of understanding it?

Consider the different forms of worship which people use today to communicate with God. Are they equally valid? Which expresses best a Christian view of the relation between God and His creation? Can a God who is wholly "other" ever be approached? Can a God who may be approached be worthy of worship?

LOCATING GOD

If we are to view God as intimately involved in His creation without being equated with it, we need a recognition that God is in one sense beyond our reach, and yet at the same time accessible to us. Two distinctions may help us to do this.

- The first distinguishes God's *transcendence* and His *immanence*. In His transcendence, God is distinct from the world, almighty and omnipotent. In His immanence, He penetrates, dwells within, and is diffused throughout His creation.
- The second comes from the Eastern Orthodox tradition and distinguishes God's *essence* and His *energies*. God's *essence* is His nature or inner being, an "otherness" which remains an incomprehensible mystery. No-one may see God face to face, although He chose to reveal Himself in the Incarnation (Ex 33:20; John 1:18). God's *energies* flow unceasingly, confirming His presence to us. His nearness to us is revealed through His acts of power.

DID GOD RETIRE?

Christians have often studied creation in the context of the debate between evolution and a literal six day creation. In that context God's creative activity is treated as a single historical event. God's continuing creative activity in the world is not acknowledged and appreciated.

By contrast, the teaching of the Eastern Orthodox Church concerning creation places a special emphasis on the fact that it is an ongoing process and contingent upon God.

"Creation is not an event in the past, but a relationship in the present... The purpose of the creation doctrine, then, is not to ascribe a chronological starting point to the world, but to affirm that at this present moment, as at all moments, the world depends for its existence upon God."

Kallistos Ware, *The Orthodox Way*

An emerging gulf

Throughout the scientific revolution the belief that God created the universe continued. Admiration and wonder at the natural world led even scientists to accept the "argument from design", belief in God as the intelligent Designer of the Universe.

But some began to see God differently. He was described in terms such as "first cause" and "distant architect". A gulf emerged between God and the world.

At the same time a mechanistic view of nature was developing. The laws of nature were thought to operate through a pre-set mechanism rather than the continuing action of God. Scientific methodologies allowed little possibility of any ongoing purpose of God being revealed through nature; scientists were primarily concerned with "how", not "why".

The romantic counter-attack

By the 19th century the Romantic movement developed, in response to people's sense that they were becoming alienated from nature through the process of industrialisation. Romanticism challenged this trend and reasserted the belief that a divine power was active in the natural world.

The movement was led in America by the philosopher Henry David Thoreau and in Britain by Romantic poets such as Wordsworth. They rejected the claim to scientific objectivity, stressing instead the interdependence of all living things. Significantly, both lived in close proximity to nature, Thoreau in a self-built house on the edge of Walden Pond and Wordsworth at Grasmere in the Lake District.

A truce?

More recently, there have been signs of a more positive and creative cross-fertilisation between science and religion.

Twentieth century scientists, especially physicists, have taken a new interest in religious questions as a result of work on relativity theory and quantum physics. Previous assumptions which separated the observer from the observed are now rejected. Scientists are recognising that the way the human mind operates affects how we perceive the nature of physical reality.

In addition, there is dissatisfaction among theologians with theories about God as a "first cause" or a powerful but remote Being who intervenes only occasionally, the kind of God once described by the former Bishop of Durham, David Jenkins, as the "divine laser beam".

James Houston argues that there is no necessary conflict between God and science as long as all events are regarded as dependent upon God's activity: "Conflict will arise only if God is assumed to be merely the God-of-the-gaps, whose activities are circumscribed to the miraculous while science studies the 'normal' or 'natural' events. If the Creator is Lord of all events, taking ultimate responsibility for everything, even evil, then the term 'natural' will not mean self-explanatory, but that fixed and stable state of processes in the universe of which God is the Ruler and Maintainer" (James Houston, *I Believe in the Creator*).

Is Process the answer?

In the twentieth century an important development has been process theology. Process theology considers reality in evolutionary terms: the process of becoming is more significant than static definitions of entities. God and the world move together through time, and He is Himself influenced by the unfolding of creation as He interacts with it. (See further pages 30-31.)

This challenges the view of God as unchanging, impassible and beyond time. This view, though often prevalent in Christian thought, was strongly influenced by Greek philosophy.

"If we are to be accurate when speaking of creation, we should use not the past tense but the continuous present. We should say, not 'God made the world, and me in it', but 'God is making the world, and me in it, here and now, at this moment and always'. Creation is not an event in the past, but a relationship in the present. If God did not continue to exert his creative will at every moment, the universe would immediately lapse into non-being; nothing could exist for a single second if God did not will it to be."

Kallistos Ware, *The Orthodox Way*

REASON AND SCRIPTURE

The idea of nature as an autonomous, self-regulating sphere, or that the universe was set in motion by a divine being but then abandoned, contradicts scripture. The Psalms in particular affirm that God's continuing involvement is necessary for the lives of creatures to be sustained (e.g. Psalm 104).

GOOD GOD GOOD WORLD

The relation between God and the world has been compared with that of an artist and a painting.

The painting reflects the character of the artist. It is external to the artist, yet the artist puts something of his or her self into the painting. They are linked through a special bond.

In the same way, the world reflects the essential goodness of God. God creates out of His love and, as love communicates goodness, He creates something which corresponds to His inner goodness. Thus the goodness of creation reflects the fact that the Creator is good.

"Christ the Incarnate One assumed flesh – organic, human flesh; he was nurtured by air and water, vegetables and meat, like the rest of us. He took matter into himself, so matter is not alien to him now. His body is a material body – transformed, of course, but transformed matter. Thus he shares his being with the whole created order."

Paulos Gregorios, in Wesley Granberg-Michaelson, *Tending the Garden*

Getting into the picture

William Temple once described Christianity as "the most materialistic of all the great religions" because, being based on the Incarnation, it "regards matter as destined to be the vehicle and instrument of spirit, and spirit as fully actual so far as it controls and directs matter."

The supreme affirmation of the value of biological life is seen in the Incarnation. As God through Christ can no longer be considered totally distinct from the world of matter, it becomes difficult to regard the material world as other than good.

Although this understanding of the Incarnation brings together matter and spirit, it is rooted in Christian orthodoxy rather than in pantheism.

Affirming matter

Many religions and philosophies are essentially negative towards the material world. In the Greek, Hindu, Gnostic and Neo-Platonic traditions, goodness is found in the realm of ideas and the soul alone is considered virtuous. The Platonists regarded matter not as evil but as unreal.

Augustine is sometimes criticised for negative attitudes to the material world, but one of his major achievements, together with the Greek Fathers of the 4th century, was to refute the argument that matter is evil.

Manicheism, a Persian religion of their day, held that there were two ultimate principles, Light and Darkness. The physical universe originated from the Darkness, while the human soul was the product of the Light. The source of evil was a second power, co-eternal with God; it was not merely the misuse of free will. Augustine responded by arguing that all earthly substances are good, and that evil is not a substance but the perversion of a nature that is essentially good.

Evil or meaningless?

Atheists sometimes argue that the presence of evil in the world makes belief in a good and sovereign God impossible. But if the presence of evil challenges the believer, the presence of good challenges the non-believer! In a novel by Elie Wiesel, a Jew whose faith has been destroyed by the Holocaust says to a rabbi, "After what has happened to us, how can you believe in God?" The rabbi replies, "How can you not believe in God after what has happened?" Even a negative experience in the world demands an explanation for the possibility of goodness.

Other people suggest that the world is not so much evil as purposeless. If the universe is merely a complex of closed systems – physical, biological and chemical – life may indeed appear to be a meaningless recurrence of natural cycles (Eccles. 1:2-11). But people's experience of goodness, an ultimate, indefinable but real awareness of quality of life, points to a positive source of power beyond these systems.

IS "NATURAL" GOOD?

"Natural equals good" is the claim of the marketing industry. Products which are said to be natural are often sold at a premium, whether it be food manufactured without additives, herbal medicines, or clothes made from organically grown cotton and coloured without chemical dyes.

But is what we consider natural always beneficial or virtuous? A final, static view of nature is a contradiction in terms. "There are only terrains and species of plants and animals known and interpreted by various cultures at different historical moments." (Rosalind Coward, *The Whole Truth*). In nature we find balance and harmony. But we also find cruelty and suffering.

Yet people make moral judgements about nature. Rousseau wrote of the "noble savage", innocent and uncorrupted by civilisation. By contrast, in a rare comment on the natural environment, Marx wrote of the "idiocy" of rural life.

In reality these judgments about nature reflect our beliefs about prevailing culture, such as the influence of technology upon nature. They also are influenced by our beliefs about the presence of the divine in nature.

The Fall means that all human beings are predisposed to sin; in this sense it is in our nature. On the other hand the sinfulness of human nature was not as God intended, and in this sense our lives are not "natural" but corrupted.

Thus, writes Kallistos Ware in *The Orthodox Way*, "There is no such thing as 'natural man' existing in separation from God. Man cut off from God is in a highly unnatural state."

GOODNESS!

How do you define "goodness"? Will that which is good in the eyes of God always seem to us to be enjoyable, attractive, and valuable?

AN OPEN-ENDED CREATION?

We can certainly sense the goodness of the natural environment, but there is also a less attractive side to nature. Co-existing with the most beautiful of creatures is the parasitic organism which causes malaria, designed with the potential to cause much suffering and with no evident good purpose. Why?

An open world?

Perhaps there is an element of freedom within the whole creation, which allows for a "dark side" to nature. This does not mean that other species have free will in the same sense as human beings have, but that there is a certain novelty and spontaneity in natural processes – and the fate of the *whole* creation is affected by the exercise of *our* will power.

If so, the world may have a certain openness as to its actual form, allowing systems to evolve which are imperfectly formed and malfunctioning. There may be a developmental aspect to the whole creation, a transformation over time which is, in fact, glorifying to God. Through such development, creation may progress in a direction which is in accordance with God's will.

From this perspective, natural processes such as disease and destructive storms can be understood as accidents in a trial-and-error process taking place over a lengthy period of time. Ultimately they may be beneficial. Minor earth tremors release tension building up in the Earth's crust, while typhoons and hurricanes redistribute the Earth's heat load more equitably.

The consequence of viewing the world in this "developmental" way is described in more detail by John Polkinghorne in *Science and Providence*.

And on the human front, if God does not compel us, it is inevitable that evil, sin and tragedy sometimes prevail. As people make new discoveries and increase their potential there are bound to be errors. Pain and suffering are in effect structured into creation. God's influence may prevail – and ultimately it certainly does – but He does not immediately and invariably overcome the not-yet-perfect products of His open creation.

An enticing God?

A theological approach has been developed (most notably in process theology) which understands God as *influencing* rather than *determining* the future. God entices or, in Alfred Whitehead's term, "lures" His creation.

Even low level matter (such as a stone) is not excluded from this process. Although the development of such an entity shows relative stability and regularity, its slow changes over time represent a response to God.

This understanding of providence and divine purpose contrasts with the pure chance of naturalism (seen in the writings of, for example, Jacques Monod and many Neo-Darwinist thinkers).

"He (God) has a vision of an ideal future, and acts to influence creatures in that direction, reacting to their deviations by presenting a new set of possibilities, leading them on."
Thomas Sieger Derr, *Ecology and Human Liberation*

Divine limitation

The more emphasis which is placed on the sovereignty of God, the less easy it is to explain the presence of evil in the world. The concept of divine limitation offers a possible resolution. Theologian Ian Barbour writes of God's "purposeful self-limitation" (*Issues in Science and Religion*).

Process theology teaches that God is intimately involved in His creation, and that the very characteristics of the world which He created limit His scope for action. God relates to His creation as One who is experimenting as much as ruling.

Critics argue that this implies a rejection of God's omnipotence and omniscience. Yet as long as there is freedom of choice, God cannot prevent evil and there must be uncertainty as to how His creation will turn out.

Might this weaken the attractiveness of God? Is the God of process theology too powerless to inspire us to worship? In facing God do we not need to experience a sense of overwhelming awe or inescapable judgement? Even a sympathiser such as Barbour suggests that in addition to the "persuasive" aspects of God we need "more active and authoritative aspects".

Yet despite this, the God of process theology maintains an appeal. If a degree of novelty and indeterminacy in creation is assumed, God can appear more sensitive to events in the world. His sovereignty is no longer likely to be confused with coercive determination. He is seeking to evoke a response which will transform the world without impinging upon its freedom. It is less easy to blame God for the prevalence of evil and suffering. Indeed He shares in the world's suffering.

How would *you* explain the justice of God and the goodness of creation, given the presence of pain and suffering in the world? Is process theology helpful, or does it raise more questions than answers?

Moltmann writes that God deliberately withdraws His presence and restricts His power to enable the possibility of freedom in His creation. This accords with the Old Testament image of God as One who does not always act to ensure the triumph of good (Josh 7.12; Judg 16:20; 1 Sam 16:14). It also accords with the cry of Christ on the cross "My God, my God, why have you forsaken me?" (Matt 27:46).

God has given the world the power to affect His activity, but He is sovereign and ultimately retains power at His disposal.

SENSING GOD'S PRESENCE

The 17th century scientists Sir Kenelm Digby, John Ray and Carl Linnaeus considered that the order and harmony in nature provided evidence of an intelligent, wise and benevolent Creator. But since that era the dualistic separation of God from the world and the spiritual from the material has affected our perception of the natural world.

People today see only the material where once they perceived the hand of God.

This situation arose partly in response to the controversies raised by Darwin. Christian thinkers reacted by reverting to a naive dualism in which the physical and biological world was assigned to science and the world of "mind" and "spirit" to religion. This "saved Christians from thinking too hard about the developing sciences and salved the consciences of the sciences who were thereby freed to get on with their work" (Arthur Peacocke).

Do you regularly – indeed have you ever – experienced the presence of God in nature? How would you describe that experience? Did you have it on a special occasion or did it come "out of the blue".

Romanticism

Romanticism was essentially a reaction to the arid intellectualism of the "Age of Reason" and the lost sense of connectedness between humankind and the rest of nature.

- The Romantics restored value to imagination, creativity, self- expression and intuition. They saw nature not as a machine but as a living companion, a source of warmth, joy, vitality and education.

- They rejected the deistic understanding of God. God was "not the external Creator of an impersonal machine, but a spirit pervading nature and known in man's own experience" (Ian G Barbour, *Issues in Science and Religion*).

God around us

In more recent times environmental philosophers and campaigners have urged a new sensitivity to nature. They believe that by becoming more aware of nature we could live in closer harmony with it and treat it with more care.

Christians have echoed that call. Theologian Sallie McFague has written in *Models of God* that if theology is to be appropriate in an age of ecological and nuclear threat, there needs to be a holistic, ecological, evolutionary view of reality and a greater appreciation of nature.

She suggests that people should not feel that they must go somewhere special (i.e. to a church) or somewhere else (i.e. another world) to sense God's presence. If our understanding of God is right, His presence should be sensed at all times and in all places: hence McFague uses the metaphor of the world as "the body of God".

Discovering God

Many people believe in a Creator at a dispassionate level as a rational explanation for the natural world. But for others it is a more emotional experience, an instinctive reaction sparked off by direct contact with nature, or even by seeing wildlife documentaries on television.

Our senses have been deadened. Yet we are aware that the wonder, beauty and power of direct contact with nature should lead us instinctively to praise God. Many of the Psalms express this experience.

We benefit by contemplating nature because it makes us more sensitive to nature.

☛ It refreshes our awareness of its intrinsic goodness and the greatness of its Creator.

☛ It offers a means of achieving wisdom and a true perspective of the place of humans in the whole creation

☛ It encourages a greater sense of environmental responsibility and motivation to act.

The world as sacrament

William Temple and, more recently, Arthur Peacocke have described the material world as a "sacrament". A sacrament is a symbol of something of spiritual significance. In Holy Communion, for example, the bread and wine are regarded as instruments or channels of God's grace.

In the sacramental model of creation this principle is extended. The material world in its entirety is considered to have a *symbolic* function, expressing God's mind and revealing His presence, and an *instrumental* function, the means whereby God's purpose is brought into effect. "The significance of the incarnation of God in a man within the created world is that in the incarnate Christ the sacramental character of that world was made explicit and perfected." (Arthur Peacocke)

"To contemplate nature is an invitation to wonder... We stand in awe of a 'power' greater than ourselves as we contemplate the infinite space and teeming complexity of life that surrounds us and has surrounded humankind from 'the beginning'."

Robert Meye

"Becoming sensitive to God's world around myself, I grow conscious also of God's world within myself. Beginning to see nature in God, I begin to see my own place as a human being within the natural order."

Kallistos Ware, *The Orthodox Way*

What is the meaning for today of God's covenant with "all living creatures of every kind" (Gen 9:16)?

HOW DO WE KNOW?

How do we know about God, and in particular how He relates to the world? How does God reveal Himself to the world?

Natural theology

Paul wrote to the Romans that "since the creation of the world God's invisible qualities – his eternal power and divine nature – have been clearly seen, being understood from what has been made, so that men are without excuse" (Rom 1:20). This is the basis of the general revelation, the belief that God discloses Himself to all through His creation.

Throughout the ages people have believed in the existence of God through the evidence of design in nature. This "natural theology" has been particularly important in Roman Catholicism.

Revealed in history

The starting point for much Protestant theology tends not to be nature but historical events (as revealed in Scripture) and personal experience.

The Bible teaches that it was the Israelites' belief that God was acting and intervening in historical events such as the Exodus, the covenant and the settlement in the Promised Land, that led them to acknowledge Him. They saw God not so much as the Creator of the world as their liberator from slavery in Egypt (Exodus 3) who moulded them as a people (Deut. 32:63).

According to Old Testament scholars their belief in God as Creator only emerged later: "From the standpoint of faith provided by Exodus and Sinai... Israelite narrators undertook the task of interpreting the whole human drama, right from the beginning" (Bernhard Anderson). Thus the God of history was also acknowledged as the Creator, and God's historical deeds were regarded as creative acts. As the Israelites viewed their salvation in the context of a process within creation, they also developed an eschatology which pointed to the renewal of all things.

The Biblical emphasis on God's action in history is partly explained by the cultural context. The Israelites were confronted in Canaan by fertility gods and goddesses, deities linked with the cycles and rhythms of the natural world (1 Kings 18). Their own God was distinct. He acted *upon* creation, using His power to intervene in history and liberate the Israelites from slavery.

Revealed through Christ

God's revelation in history and nature is brought together in the work of Christ. The gospel of John, the epistle of Paul to the Colossians and the book of Hebrews describe how all things were made in and through Christ (John 1:1-3; Col 1:15-20; Heb 1:2-3). Christ is portrayed as the mediator of God acting in creation. His mastery of the forces of nature in miracles may be seen as a sign that the natural world is incorporated into salvation history.

The ultimate meaning of creation is not that the natural world provides a theatre upon which the history of men and women is staged, as suggested by Karl Barth. The Bible does not distinguish history and nature. It reveals that God acts in both. History points to a new, consummated creation.

"God's revelation in creation is not verbal; its message does not come to us in human language. 'They have no speech, there are no words,' writes David of the heavens telling the glory of God (Ps 19.3). Mankind has in large measure lost the capacity to interpret what the heavens are saying in their wordless message. The Scriptures, on the other hand, are couched in the words of ordinary human discourse... They are plain in a way that general revelation never is, have a 'perspicuity' that is not found in the book of nature. In a way, therefore, the Scriptures are like a verbal commentary on the dimly perceived sign language of creation."
Albert Wolters, *Creation Regained*

GOD'S CREATIVE EXPRESSION

God continually expresses Himself through creative activity in nature. The Bible describes this activity in three ways: God acting through His will, His word and His wisdom.

God's will

God determined that there should be a creation through His will. Creation did not take place arbitrarily, by chance or necessity, but by a loving act of willpower. "Nothing compelled him to create; he chose to do so. The world was not created unintentionally or out of necessity; it is not an automatic emanation or overflowing from God, but the consequence of divine choice" (Kallistos Ware, *The Orthodox Way*).

There is nothing "outside" of God from which He creates life. But instead of saying that God made the universe out of "nothing", it is more meaningful to say that He creates it out of His own self, which is love, for loving demands sharing.

In *God in Creation* Jurgen Moltmann describes God's creative resolve as an act of will which, initially, is directed inwards – before acting God determines that He is to be the world's Creator.

Neither is life created from an innate ability of living materials to reproduce using mechanisms entirely governed by chance, a theory put forward by the molecular biologist Jacques Monod in his classic study *Chance and Necessity*. Monod adopted his scientific findings relating to the randomness of genetic mutations and raised them to the level of a metaphysical principle governing the whole universe. His theory contradicts evidence of an underlying purpose and fails to explain adequately the development out of primeval matter of richly varied life-systems.

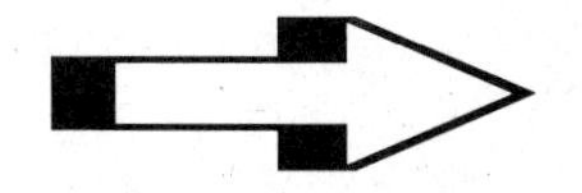

GOING FURTHER

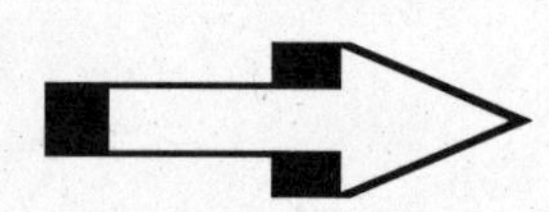

God's word

The word of God is frequently used in the Bible as a description of God's creative expression. It forms a continuum, joining the Creator and His creation: "God's will is spoken, and with His speech the deed is done" (James Houston).

Through this Word all things are sustained (Heb 1:3, cf. Deut 8:3), and God structures and fills creation. As God speaks, His will is revealed and His Word releases a power which sustains creation, shapes people's lives and affects the course of history.

God's wisdom

God creates through His wisdom. This is suggested in particular in Proverbs, where wisdom is personified and described as the first of the works of God, the craftsman at His side (Prov 8:22-30).

Wisdom in the Bible is not an abstract principle or ideal, but an illumination of God's will and a reflection of His character. It is attainable not by self-improvement but as a gift from "the only wise God" (Prov 2:6, Rom 16:27). Whoever finds wisdom, finds life (Prov 8:35). And in Christ "are hidden all the treasures of wisdom and knowledge" (Col 2:3).

"Divine disclosure is related to the realities of daily life, transcendence is linked to immanence. The living presence of the Word made flesh enables us to be wise in all aspects of reality" (James M Houston, *I Believe in the Creator*).

Additional reading

The most important theological text is Jurgen Moltmann's *God in Creation*, which is challenging but rewarding. Kallistos Ware's *The Orthodox Way* contains many penetrating insights. Sallie McFague's *Models of God* is controversial but worthy of study. See also the chapter by Robert Meye in Wesley Granberg-Michaelson's *Tending the Garden*.

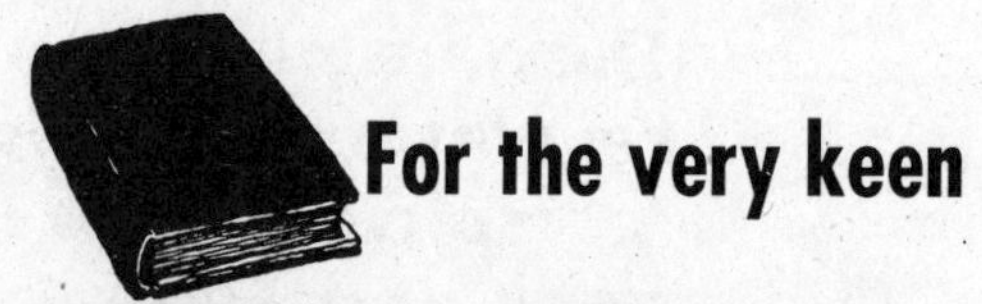

For the very keen

John Polkinghorne, *Science and Providence*, Chapters 1-5
John Polkinghorne sets out to establish that a God in continual interaction with all creation is a credible concept in a scientific age. Is Polkinghorne's attempt to find God "in the process" as distinct from "in the gaps" successful? How satisfactorily does he define the possibility of a deity who allows freedom within the universe and yet has scope for His own activity?

Sallie McFague, *Models of God*, Chapters 4-6
An important attempt by a liberal theologian to develop alternatives to the traditional imperialistic imagery for God. Do you find the models of God as Mother, Lover and Friend to be credible, appropriate and imaginative?

Jurgen Moltmann, *God in Creation*, Chapters 1 & 4
The most significant development of creation theology in modern times. Does Moltmann's description of God as a personal and participatory power in creation conflict with the concept of God's immutability?

Paulos Gregorios, *The Human Presence*, Chapters 5 & 6
An influential Eastern Orthodox response to the ecology crisis. How would you evaluate the concept of humans as mediators between God and the cosmos?

SUSTAINING THE EARTH

UNIT 4

THE HUMAN FACTOR

CONTENTS

PURPOSE

The purpose of this Unit is to explore what the Bible teaches about our human responsibilities for the created world, in particular how we are to be "stewards" of the environment.

KING OF THE JUNGLE

Are all species equally important and equally valuable? Or should human beings in some sense be considered higher than other species?

The fact that we see our species as superior to others is frequently blamed for the destructive impact human beings have had on the environment.

- Throughout the Middle Ages this view of humanity prevailed and was defended on theological grounds.
- During the Enlightenment it was reinforced by the quest for human autonomy.
- As science developed it was justified on the basis of our physical differences and greater mental capabilities.

A part or apart?

During the industrial revolution, belief in human superiority reinforced people's sense of separation from the natural environment.

As people became alienated from nature, they objectified it as the world "out there". It was regarded as an expansive external area of infinite possibilities to explore, control and dominate.

Thus an essential link between human beings and the rest of creation was weakened. People increasingly saw themselves as *apart from* nature rather than *a part of* nature.

Unique, so responsible

Christianity has been blamed for causing arrogance, because of the emphasis it has traditionally placed on the unique capacities of human beings.

But the other side of the coin is that the uniqueness of humanity places upon us a special responsibility to care for other species. Our capabilities, such as moral awareness, make our abuse of other species all the more worthy of condemnation. The Bible is not slow to point this out (e.g. Prov 12:10).

Human dominion

The author of Genesis states clearly the place of human beings in the natural order: "Then God said, 'Let us make man in our image, in our likeness, and let them rule over the fish of the sea and the birds of the air, over the livestock, over all the earth, and over all the creatures that move along the ground'" (Gen 1:26). Human beings were to have dominion over – to rule over – the Earth (Gen 1:28).

The Psalmist is similarly forthright about the place of human beings: "You made him a little lower than the heavenly beings and crowned him with glory and honour. You made him ruler over the works of your hands; you put everything under his feet" (Ps 8:5-6).

One of the distinct features of a Christian environmental ethic is that our use of other species is clearly sanctioned. The Hebrew term used for "rule over", *radah*, is forceful, derived from a verb which means "trample".

Godly kingship

But dominion is not to be confused with domination or unrestrained licence. God puts limits on human activity. Human dominion is qualified, as "God is the King of all the earth" (Ps 47:7). What, then, is meant by dominion?

The Bible indicates that dominion involves service to others. There is a sense of authority, but this is not to be abused. Thus when Adam is told to "work" the garden of Eden, the Hebrew term used is *abad*, which also means to serve (Gen 2:15). Dominion as a form of servanthood is also seen in the life of Jesus (e.g. Matt 20:28, Phil 2:6,7).

Dominion also involves restraint. It was a duty of Israel's kings neither to accumulate wealth nor to consider themselves better than fellow Israelites (Deut 17:14-20).

Elsewhere in the Bible ruling over others is linked with shepherding (2 Sam 5:2, Matt 2:6, John 10:11). Shepherds do not merely exploit their sheep. They watch over, protect and care for them.

Stewards of God's land

Much Christian teaching concerning the environment, from Benedictine to Calvinist, has been based on a model of stewardship. Human beings are seen as stewards of a world which is the property of the Creator (Lev 25:23, Ps 24:1).

The stewardship model has many merits. But critics argue that it separates God, humankind and nature. It implies that God is absent and the land is "out there". The idea of stewardship, they suggest, will not prevent nature from being objectified as property intended for human use, any more than the idea of dominion.

Friends of the earth?

Perhaps an alternative model is needed. Church of Scotland theologian Ruth Page suggests that this might be based on "companionship".

Companionship does not imply dominance or ownership. Instead it conveys a sense of shared interest, a recognition that one part of the natural world needs other parts in order to function properly. It thus highlights the interdependence of living things, which is a key ecological concept.

What do you think are the advantages and disadvantages of the concepts of dominion, stewardship and companionship in describing the relationship between God, humankind and the rest of nature?

THE CALL TO RESTRAINT

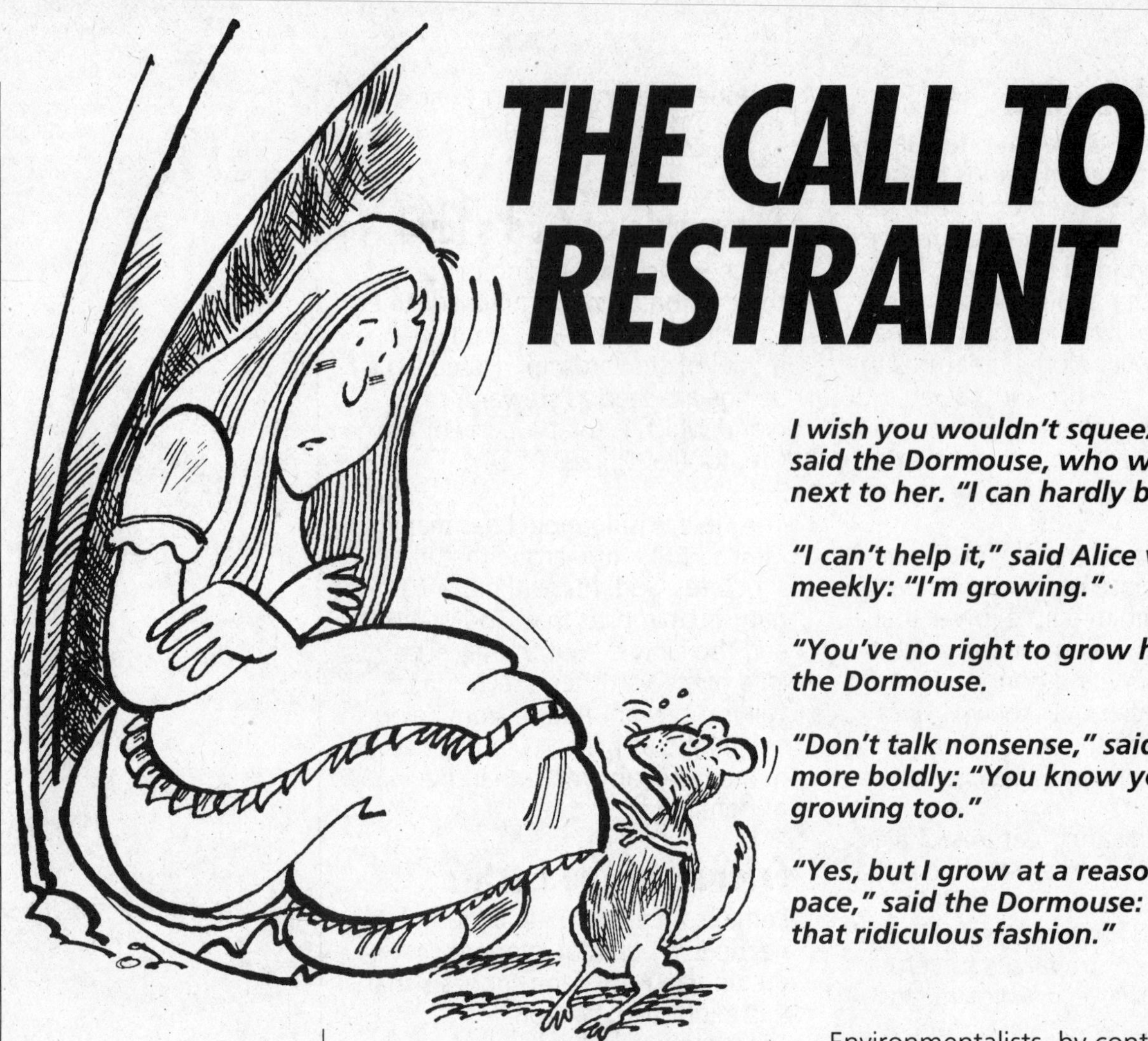

I wish you wouldn't squeeze so," said the Dormouse, who was sitting next to her. "I can hardly breathe."

"I can't help it," said Alice very meekly: "I'm growing."

"You've no right to grow here," said the Dormouse.

"Don't talk nonsense," said Alice more boldly: "You know you're growing too."

"Yes, but I grow at a reasonable pace," said the Dormouse: "not in that ridiculous fashion."

In the mid-1970s John Taylor, then Bishop of Winchester, produced a popular book called *Enough is Enough*. It began with that extract from *Alice in Wonderland*. In criticising post-war consumerism Bishop Taylor sought to develop a "theology of enough", urging people to avoid the excesses which he believed were causing environmental degradation.

What is progress?

Progress is too often confused with affluence. Economists and politicians tend to define our standard of living according to the rate at which economic output grows.

Environmentalists, by contrast, have argued that the rate of economic growth is a poor indicator of our quality of life. Alternative models of development and indicators of "progress" are needed.

The concept of "sustainable development", popularised through the Brundtland Report, *Our Common Future*, is a helpful guiding principle. Sustainable development "meets the needs of the present without compromising the ability of future generations to meet their own needs." Sustainable development is, however, interpreted in many different ways.

The report's authors argued that sustainable development allows for increased consumption in industrialised countries. But many environmentalists believe that if non-renewable resources are not to be unduly depleted and total world energy consumption is to be sustainable, increased consumption is only permissible in less industrialised countries which suffer from widespread poverty.

ECO-LOGY AND ECO-NOMICS

The word "economics" means the *management* of our surroundings (or, strictly speaking, "house"). "Ecology" is the *study* of these surroundings.

Perhaps it is not without significance that economics is a long-established academic discipline, whereas popular interest in ecology is relatively recent.

The dominance of economics over ecology in stature suggests that the cart has been put before the horse. Is it surprising, then, that politicians have tended to place economic targets before environmental goals?

The Biblical pattern

In warning against self-indulgence and greed, the Bible calls for restraint in our use of the Earth. The exercise of restraint is regarded in the Bible as a form of wisdom: "Do not wear yourself out to get rich; have the wisdom to show restraint" (Prov 23:4). Wisdom is identified with knowledge of creation (1 Kings 4:29-34).

Ecclesiastes refers to the need to find a balance between folding our hands and "chasing after the wind" (Ecc 4:5-6). Likewise Paul, writing to Timothy, considered that bare essentials such as food and clothing should suffice (1 Tim 6:8).

From the very beginning God imposed limits on our consumption. The creation is described as "good", but Adam and Eve are told that they may only eat seed-bearing plants and fruit. No sanction for eating meat is given until after the Fall and Flood (Gen 1:29-30 cf. Gen 9:3).

Many Old Testament laws encouraged restraint. The Fourth Commandment, to rest on the Sabbath, is one example. The Sabbath applies not only to people but to animals (Ex 20:8-11). And the principle of Sabbath rest was also to apply to the land – every seventh year it was to be left unploughed and unused (Lev 25:4).

Slower growth

The economic output of the Israelite's agrarian economy would have been less as a result of such laws. Agricultural productivity would have been lowered by the practice of not harvesting edges of fields and not revisiting vines or sheaves which had been neglected (Lev 19:9-10, Deut 24:19).

And rules concerning debt and interest may well have had the effect of preventing financial speculation and the accumulation of capital (Deut 15:1, Lev 25:35-7). These are traditionally considered essential for economic growth.

The benefits of restraint

So why is restraint demanded?

❶ To protect the fecundity of the earth.

Sensitivity to the laws of nature is just common sense. The Israelites were instructed not to eat fruit from newly planted trees in the first three years in order to improve future harvests (Lev 19:23-25).

❷ To avoid making an idol of material wealth.

The quest for ever-increasing material wealth is a form of idolatry. Jesus warned: "No-one can serve two masters" (Matt 6:24). The story of the rich young man teaches that the possession of wealth obstructs people from wholehearted commitment to God (Luke 18:18-30).

❸ To reduce injustice.

The accumulation of wealth all too often results in injustice and exploitation of the weak. Moses was told to prevent any sale of land which resulted in one party taking advantage of another (Lev 25:14). Buying up land and joining it together into large estates was condemned (Is 5:8).

❹ To discourage wrongful desires.

Developing an attitude of restraint helps us overcome our tendency to covet (to desire wrongfully) the property of other people (Ex 20:17). It helps us to resist envy.

Less, or just different?

Despite the growth of environmental concern, most people are very resistant to the idea of reducing their consumption. Many individuals don't act because they feel that their action will not by itself make any difference.

The emergence of "green consumerism" has had a significant impact on the market. But some argue that it does not° go far enough. People are only encouraged to change the type of products which they purchase, not to reduce their consumption.

"'Progress' is no longer an expression of hope, as it was in the nineteenth century. It is a fate to which people in the industrial countries feel condemned."

Jurgen Moltmann, *God in Creation*

Identify four passages in the Bible where wealth is portrayed as an obstacle to people's relationship to God. Are there other passages which portray wealth as a sign of God's favour? If so, can you reconcile them?

THINK!

Is it realistic to expect a modern, free society to curtail advertising, consumer debt and Sunday trading? Should the exercise of restraint be left to individual choice or promoted by government measures?

WHERE WILL IT ALL END?

If the Earth is ultimately destined for destruction, why should we bother to devote great energy to caring for it? After all, the Bible ends with the promise of a *new* earth (Rev 21:1).

Discarded or recycled?

The Bible's teaching about the last things ("eschatology") is not easily understood. Different expectations about the ultimate fate of the Earth have been derived from the text of Scripture.

In the Bible there are contrasting images of the future.

- **Isaiah** sees future salvation as the whole creation dwelling in harmony: wolves lying alongside lambs, lions eating straw like oxen (Is 11:6-9). Such a picture is also contained in Paul's letters to the Romans, Colossians and Ephesians, which point to a renewal of all things in creation (Rom 8:21, Col 1:20, Eph 1:10).
- **Peter** seems to suggest that the material world is to be destroyed (2 Pet 3:10). An "otherworldly" dimension to Christianity is also apparent in the writings of John and in the epistle to the Hebrews (John 17:28, Heb 12:27).

These different interpretations are reflected in the writings of theologians. Paul Santmire subtitled his book *The Travail of Nature* "the ambiguous ecological promise of Christian theology." He identifies some theologians who have anticipated the final negation of matter (Origen, Aquinas, Teilhard de Chardin) and others who have predicted some kind of re-fashioning and glorifying of the material world (Irenaeus, Francis, Augustine).

Santmire is critical of modern Protestant theology which "has generally given little or no substantive thought to the eschatological future of nature." He points out that the influential twentieth century theologian, Karl Barth, depicts the scene of eternity as essentially a landless event.

"We shall in the future world see the material forms of the new heavens and the new earth in such a way that we shall most distinctly recognise God everywhere and governing all things, material as well as spiritual."

St. Augustine

Each of us applies an interpretative framework when reading the Bible. We decide, consciously or otherwise, which parts of the Bible are pivotal. We prioritise some parts over others.

In reading Biblical passages about the end times, we should be guided by an understanding of the historical context, be faithful to the original text, and apply the teaching carefully to the contemporary setting.

Bearing all that in mind, how would *you* interpret what the Bible says about the end times? Are we heading for harmony or destruction?

Back to nothing?

One theological model for considering the future of the material world tries to see a symmetry in the beginning and end of time. "Our thinking about how and why God created the world carries implications for what God's relationship to the Earth is now, and what it ultimately will be." (Wesley Granberg-Michaelson, *A Worldly Spirituality*)

Some Christians envisage a kind of return to the paradise setting of the Garden of Eden. Others argue that the Earth will finally be abrogated, returned to nothing.

The doctrine of *creatio ex nihilo* (creation out of nothing) is not explicit in the Bible. It arose out of the early church's concern that dualism was being perpetuated through ideas rooted in Greek philosophy.

The Greeks believed in a realm of ideal, spiritual, ordering forces which were good, and contrasted this with the ever-changing material world, which they regarded as evil. The world was self-sufficient and self-sustaining, with no beginning and no end. Matter was eternally in existence alongside God.

By contrast, in the Hebrew tradition the world was sustained by continual reference to God. A linear progression in history led from creation to consummation. But this left some uncertainty as to whether God *made* or merely *formed* the material world. The church thus developed the doctrine of "creation out of nothing" to affirm that God was sole Creator of all things and that everything was created good.

"Declaring that God made the world from nothing seems to fit well with modern notions of the world's autonomy: made from nothing, the world is connected to nothing outside of itself"

Wesley Granberg-Michaelson, *A Worldly Spirituality*

Some Christians question the validity of this doctrine. According to Granberg-Michaelson, it reinforces the assumption that God is separate from creation. There is an alternative understanding – that God did not create the universe out of "nothing" but out of Himself (page 25).

The end is nigh

Street evangelists have traditionally urged people to repent because of the imminence of the end of the world. Even aside from the fact that "no-one knows about that day or hour, not even the angels in heaven, nor the Son" (Matt 24.36), this is an unfortunate approach to evangelism. It leads people into a faith which has a dismissive view of the importance of the material world.

According to Moltmann "the expectation of 'the end of the world' is a vulgar error." There are better motives than fear for leading people to become Christians. The positive prospect of the transformation of the material world could equally inspire people to faith.

LESSONS FOR HUMANS

Scientists estimate that there are at least 5 million species on Earth and possibly as many as 30 million. Many are under threat through the destruction of habitats, pollution, exploitation, or the introduction of alien species.

The most biologically diverse areas are in the tropics; tropical rainforests probably contain 50% of all species on Earth. Many of our medicines, as well as timber, rubber, oils, lubricants and a host of other products, originate there.

In the beginning the natural state of the Earth was to bear fruit. The blessing of God showered down upon the whole creation, including humankind. The Israelites were instructed that the land belonged to God, who would teach them how to use it and expected them to take good care of it (Gen 2:15, Lev 25:23, Ps 24:1, Is 28:24-6).

Vulnerability

The fact that all living species are interconnected means that human wellbeing is linked to the fate of the Earth. We form part of a living community of species. Harming other species in the community is thus like threatening to cut off our personal life-support system.

We share an inherent vulnerability with all other forms of life. We are mortal (Gen 6:3). Isaiah describes people as like grass (Is 40:6-8). We need to acknowledge our weakness before the Creator. As Job said, after God described His majestic power over creation: "Surely I spoke of things I did not understand, things too wonderful for me to know" (Job 42:3).

Is obedience enough?

There are many laws of cause and effect in nature which are self- evident. Taking good care of the environment will enable it to remain fruitful.

But taking account of these laws and, specifically, the small number of practical rules about the environment in the Bible, may not be enough. The Old Testament makes it clear that the response of people to God and the fertility of the land are linked in a much broader sense.

The natural environment is affected by the rebellion of God's people. As a consequence of the Israelites' disobedience "even the land was defiled; so I punished it for its sin" (Lev 18:25). The land was made barren not because of bad stewardship, but due to a host of other sins. When the Israelites' land was affected by disease, Moses explained that it was because they had broken the covenant and worshipped other gods (Deut 29:22-8).

Deuteronomy 11, 28
Leviticus 26

The *blessings* for obeying God are:

- a fruitful womb
- crops from the land
- calves and lambs
- victory over enemies
- seasonal rain
- a healthy economy

The *curses* for disobedience are:

- disease and fever
- defeat by enemies
- soil that will not yield crops
- trees that will not yield fruit
- wild animals that attack children and animals
- oppression and robbery

In the Old Testament environmental problems are predicted for reasons other than bad management practices. God intervenes with blessings or curses in accordance with people's response to Him.

How applicable is this teaching to the modern era? Is it invariably true that when we are faithful to God our material needs will be met and we will live in peace? And that when we turn from God we will get ecological disaster and social oppression?

An uncertain future

During the past thirty years fears of environmental catastrophe have increased markedly. But concern at environmental problems and the quality of life can be traced back to the Romantic poets and political philosophers such as John Stuart Mill and William Morris.

Sometimes fears about the future have proved excessive. In the 18th century Thomas Malthus concluded that there was a tendency in nature for population to outstrip all possible means of subsistence and warned that the future was very bleak.

Like any predictions, environmental forecasts are subject to many variables. How long non-renewable resources last will depend on future discoveries. Even current reserves are not easily quantified. Resource prices will change, affecting the extent to which extraction is "economic". Innovative design and microtechnology may reduce the volume of raw materials required in products.

Reversing the trend

Today we have unprecedented power to destroy life on Earth on a huge scale. Sometimes environmental degradation is not immediately apparent. We may need to apply the "precautionary principle" – to take early steps to reduce the risk of damage even though scientific proof is not yet available.

But if we have this power, it follows that we can also reverse the trend towards the destruction of the planet. What lessons can we learn from our faith?

Waiting for God

God alone will determine the end time. It is not for us to determine when this present world will "end". The disciples expected Jesus to return very soon after his ascension (James 5:8). We are taught simply to live as if he will return at any moment (Matt 24:42-4). It is certainly not our right, or our calling, to bring forward the destruction of the Earth by abuse of the natural environment.

A response to environmental degradation is needed at both a personal and structural level. We need to change our lifestyles so that they cause the least possible environmental damage. This has implications for our use of energy, land and other resources, our purchases, our investments and so forth.

We also have a duty to address structural issues such as the impact of economic policies, the role of industry, and values taught in our educational system. Such practical concerns will be explored in the final two Units of this course.

GOING FURTHER

A covenant responsibility

Environmental catastrophe is foreshadowed early in the Bible with the story of Noah. God made a covenant never again to destroy the Earth in a flood. A "covenant" is an agreement, or pledge, through which relationships are regulated so that they work effectively. Significantly, the covenant was not only with Noah but with "every living creature" and "all generations to come" (Gen 9:12).

Later, on Mount Sinai a new covenant was made between God and the Israelites. God declared that they were a special nation to Him and that their obedience would be rewarded with His blessing in the form of healthy crops and freedom from drought and disease (Ex 19:5-6).

Human dominion over the Earth is qualified by our covenant responsibilities. If we obey the Creator, we will enjoy the fruit of the earth. In understanding the drama of creation "one is continually brought up against the fact that morality, response to God, and fertility of the earth are interrelated" (William Dyrness in *Tending the Garden*). In other words, human faithfulness will result in earthly fertility. Indeed, Dyrness suggests, the very stability of the created order appears in a sense dependent upon the Israelites' faithfulness.

Additional reading

Tending the Garden, by Wesley Granberg-Michaelson (ed), has two chapters relevant to this unit, by William Dyrness and Paulos Mar Gregorios. Economist Herman Daly and theologian John Cobb have written a major text bringing together economics and ecology, *For the Common Good*. Wesley Granberg-Michaelson's *A Worldly Spirituality* contains a chapter on Christian views on the future of the world and the second coming. A key text on process theology is John Cobb and Charles Birch *Liberating Life*. A useful all round book, though written from an American perspective, is Loren Wilkinson (ed), *Earthkeeping in the 90s*.

For the very keen

Ronald J Sider, *Rich Christians in an Age of Hunger*
A classic study of Christian responsibility towards the poor. Many Christians argue that the fate of the poor is more important than the fate of the environment. What sources of poverty does Sider identify which suggest that neither can be solved in isolation from the other?

Brian Griffiths, *Morality and the Market Place*
Professor Griffiths, formerly policy adviser to Mrs Thatcher, outlines alternatives to capitalism and socialism. Griffiths believes that a humanist philosophy has led people to believe that "the creation of wealth is of less concern and morally inferior than its distribution" (p 124). Elsewhere he argues that "the order to create wealth can never justify permanent damage to the balance of nature" (p 92). Do you find these statements consistent?

H Paul Santmire, *The Travail of Nature*, Chapters 7, 8 & 10
A systematic and historical study of theologians' attitudes to nature. Consider the evidence for Santmire's claim that "modern Protestant theology has generally given little or no substantive thought to the eschatological future of nature" (p 140). Does Santmire's 'ecological reading of the Bible' suggest that more weight can be given to particular Scriptural passages at different times in history?

SUSTAINING THE EARTH

UNIT 5

GREENING THE GREY MATTER

CONTENTS

PURPOSE

The purpose of this Unit is to explore the range of beliefs and philosophies held by environmentalists.

MORE THAN A SCIENCE

We have already seen that ecology cannot be reduced to science (see page 8). If ecology is "the study of the structure and function of nature", then it will certainly be informed by scientific findings. But people within the environmental movement hold a range of beliefs. These beliefs are rooted in scientific evidence, but go beyond it and try to make *sense* of the world.

But what is ecology, then? Can it be properly described as a philosophy? Is ecology a "world view"? Or even a new religion? Before considering particular beliefs held by environmentalists, some of these terms need to be clarified. How do we distinguish between faith, world views, and philosophies?

The roots of our beliefs

Our **world view** guides how we perceive the world around us, how we interpret it, and how we orientate ourselves to live in it. It arises out of our assumptions concerning the basic make-up of the world, the fundamental beliefs which we share with those around us and which shape our vision of life.

These fundamental beliefs are essentially religious, because they reflect what we deem worthy of ultimate concern and devotion. They are held on the basis of a personal commitment, or **faith**. Albert Wolters defines a world view as a "life-perspective" which is "a matter of shared everyday experience". A world view is thus practical, personal, culturally influenced, and rooted in faith.

Philosophy involves the exploration of ideas and arguments and the ordering of thought into a coherent framework. It contains several branches of study, including metaphysics (investigating the nature of reality from first principles) and axiology (the study of values in, for example, morality, art and politics). Metaphysics can itself be subdivided into epistemology (the study of knowledge) and ontology (the study of being).

Philosophy thus provides a theoretical view of the totality of reality. It may be subdivided into subject areas or academic disciplines (such as ecology) which consider limited aspects of reality (such as relationships within nature).

Interactions

Our personal commitments are the crucial driving force behind our thought processes. Our world view underlies our philosophy.

At the same time, how we think will shape our world view and our faith. The relationship is circular. The distinctions are not sharp, but broadly we could say that:

- **philosophy differs from faith** in that it is less committed and more theoretical. It can be speculative, transient, partial and tentative.
- **a world view differs from philosophy** in being pre-theoretical. It is expressed through philosophy by the use of models and analogies.

DEFINITIONS

World view: a pre-theoretical view of the totality of reality

Philosophical paradigm: a theoretical view of the totality of reality

Academic discipline: a theoretical view of a particular aspect of reality

Ecology as world view

So where does ecology fit in? It certainly has a philosophical dimension. But some in the environmental movement see ecology as *more* than a philosophy. They believe that the philosophical method of rational enquiry is too limiting to be the only way of determining how to live, and point to the importance of intuition in arriving at truth and knowledge.

It is possible to make ecology the basis of a world view, one which will guide how we perceive and orientate ourselves in the world. According to Edward Goldsmith, editor of *The Ecologist*, ecology was the world view of the 18th century natural theologians, of Goethe, Wordsworth and the other Romantic poets, of Thoreau and Leopold, and of the early academic ecologists such as Clements and Shelford and (later) Allee and the Chicago School.

"Ecology is above all a world view or social paradigm. It has been the world view of traditional peoples from time immemorial – this is why they never destroyed their natural environment and their societies displayed such incredible stability and continuity."

Edward Goldsmith, *The Way* (an attempt to develop a fully integrated world view based on ecology)

Is ecology a religion?

Awareness of the interconnectedness of all things is a key defining feature of an ecological world view. To be ecologically conscious entails "a realization that we are an extension of nature and nature an extension of us" (Henryk Skolimowski, *Eco-Philosophy*). But this is a *metaphysical* claim, a claim about the nature of reality, and implies a prior faith commitment.

This "realization" of our interconnectedness might be rooted in a belief that all life can ultimately be reduced to one category - that, in essence, all life is one. In this case the underlying faith commitment is to pantheistic monism.

Alternatively, the realization might be rooted in a belief that humankind is made from the Earth and shares with all other beings a dependence on the Spirit of God for life. This would reflect a faith commitment to Christianity (Gen 2:7, Ps 104:30).

Ecology itself is therefore *not* a religion, although it can form the basis of philosophical beliefs which are then underpinned by religious commitment. Indeed different ecological philosophers perceive the world differently *because* they hold divergent beliefs about the existence and nature of God:

- **Christian theists** believe that God acts through the world and yet exists beyond it.
- **Deists** see the world as created by a god who exists entirely separately from it and can be understood without special revelation.
- **Pagans** believe that the Earth is the outward manifestation of a deity and full of spirit beings.
- **Pantheists** identify God with the universe and see within it an underlying unity.
- **Humanists** deny the existence of a deity and see humankind at the centre of purpose and meaning in life.

Everyone holds beliefs arrived at through faith. And faith operates at a deeper level than the rational ordering of our thoughts.

A PHILOSOPHY FOR LIFE

Ecological philosophy may be defined as the application of philosophical methods to the study of ecology. It involves exploring ideas concerning the structure and function of nature, and ordering them into a coherent framework.

There is more than one philosophical approach to ecology. "Green philosophy", the school of thought associated with *Small is Beautiful* author E.F. Schumacher, has strongly influenced radical environmental campaigners.

Knowing our place

In order to explore ecology in depth it is ultimately necessary to address metaphysical questions relating to the cosmic order. This requires us to define the relationship between human beings and nature.

- Do we understand reality better by regarding ourselves as part of nature, or as separate from it?
- Do we have the freedom to dominate and exploit nature, or should we allow ourselves to live at the mercy of natural forces?
- In rethinking the relationship between human beings and nature, is it necessary to abandon the mechanistic conception of the world?

Schumacher criticised the philosophies of relativism and positivism which have been dominant since the 19th century, and concluded that there was a need for "metaphysical reconstruction":

"While the nineteenth century ideas deny or obliterate the hierarchy of levels in the universe, the notion of an hierarchical order is an indispensable instrument of understanding. Without the recognition of 'Levels of Being' or 'Grades of Significance' we cannot make the world intelligible to ourselves nor have we the slightest possibility to define our own position, the position of man, in the scheme of the universe."
E F Schumacher *Small is Beautiful*

Knowing our values

Likewise, ecological study involves axiological questions – questions about values. There is a practical need to make moral, aesthetic and political judgements about the value of our surroundings.

- Is it immoral to experiment on animals?
- Is wilderness more visually attractive than cultivated land?
- On what basis should a community decide whether to allow the building of a new retail complex on a green field site?

The study of relationships may assist in answering such questions. But we also need a coherent metaphysical understanding before we can address moral issues adequately.

Not all environmentalists adopt the same approach to nature, or have the same motives. Some people's concern for the environment is essentially utilitarian. They believe there is a need to protect the environment simply in order to maximise their present enjoyment of it. Other people are motivated by an idealism which lead to a concern for future generations or the wellbeing of other species.

Likewise some believe that nature is instructive, others that nature is ambiguous. Observation of other species could lead people to adopt either a co-operative or competitive approach to life. Studying nature does not necessarily lead to a desire for harmony between species. It might lead some people to a belief in the need to exert control over nature.

Eco-philosophy

Henryk Skolimowski, Professor of Philosophy at the University of Michigan, has been one of the major contemporary influences on ecological philosophy. He has called for "a new philosophy which actually marks a return to the great tradition of philosophy – the tradition that takes upon itself large tasks and attempts to be culturally significant" (*Eco-philosophy*).

Pythagoras defined philosophy as the knowledge of things human and divine. It was only later that philosophy was limited to matters of reason. Skolimowski similarly defines philosophy broadly, and believes that it should influence every element of social, individual, spiritual, ecological and political life.

Skolimowski contrasts the characteristics of Eco-philosophy with contemporary philosophy. Key elements of Eco-philosophy are that it is:

- life-oriented
- spiritually alive
- comprehensive and global
- environmentally and ecologically conscious
- aligned with the economics of the quality of life
- tolerant of transphysical phenomena

Eco-Reality

According to Skolimowski, there are "fields of interacting forces" between people and their surroundings which need to be kept in equilibrium. Our health depends on the well being of the planet and we must therefore recognise the sanctity of life.

The whole cosmos is evolving. Detached and objective study is impossible: we arrive at meaning when we "compassionately unite ourselves with the larger flow of life."

Human beings have a spiritual dimension. We need to try to grasp the stars, even if only to understand where our feet are. This quest for meaning differentiates us from other species.

Eco-Knowledge

Skolimowski argues that empirical methods based on the mechanistic view of the world have failed. They cannot, for example, explain complementary medicine or paranormal phenomena. There is thus a need to be open to the possibility of other means of knowing.

People already have a vast amount of knowledge. But we lack wisdom: discernment in the selective application of knowledge. This should be based on "our understanding of the awesome and fragile fabric of life."

Eco-Values

Skolimowski believes that we need to integrate into economics an awareness of other forms of value which make up the "quality of life".

He rejects individualism. Society is "the nexus and cradle of aspirations and visions... one of the modes of man's spiritual being."

Roots

Skolimowski's ecological world view is rooted in humanism. He regards ideas of God as images and symbols which people have deified and institutionalised to help them in their spiritual journeys. In other words, we have made God in our own image. Spirituality is "an instrument of the perfectibility of man." But people who share a similar world view may do so from a different basis of faith.

"All philosophy has only one justification, the enhancement of life."
Henryk Skolimowski, *Eco-philosophy*

SOME GREEN INFLUENCES

BACKGROUND

Over the past thirty years a growing multitude of campaigning groups have tried to reduce the level of environmental damage. They range from large international organisations such as Greenpeace to small local groups opposed to building developments. Green political parties have been established in many countries, over a dozen of which have gained representation in national parliaments.

The underlying philosophy of this green movement has been shaped by the writings of (among others) E.F. Schumacher, Ivan Illich, Fritjof Capra, Murray Bookchin, Arne Naess and Jonathon Porritt. All have drawn attention to the fractured relationship between humankind and the environment in modern industrialised world. Their ideas form part of a tradition of social critics, dissidents, poets and philosophers who have argued that the costs of industrialisation often outweigh the benefits.

Romantic poets

The 19th century Romantic poets such as Wordsworth, Coleridge and Shelley observed the urban squalor and degradation of the natural environment which were the result of industrialisation. They regarded nature as beautiful, inspiring and healing, and mourned the loss of human empathy with it. They believed that direct contact with nature provided an opportunity for spiritual regeneration and an education that could not be received in any other way.

American transcendentalists

The Romantic tradition was also evident in America, where it surfaced in the latter part of the 19th century in the writings of Thoreau, Emerson and Muir. In the present century the American conservationist Aldo Leopold has been an important influence. Leopold developed the idea of a "land ethic", through which people see the land as a "community" to which they belong.

Mill

Liberal philosopher John Stuart Mill's critique of Victorian society a century ago has been a strong influence on today's ecological economists such as Herman Daly. Mill was highly critical of the prevailing economic system which meant that "the normal state of human beings is that of struggling to get on... trampling, crushing, elbowing and treading on each other's heels." Mill called instead for "the stationary state of capital and wealth", today more accurately described as a "steady state economy", where people would be concerned with the "Art of Living" rather than the accumulation of riches.

Schweitzer

Dismayed at the loss of idealistic attitudes towards life, missionary and Protestant pastor Albert Schweitzer developed an ethical principle which he summed up as "reverence for life". This was essentially a belief that it is good to maintain and encourage life and bad to destroy life or obstruct it. Schweitzer believed that life should be treated as sacred. Though he recognised that some damage to life was inevitable in the course of human activity, our moral responsibility was to minimise this.

Whitehead

Twentieth century philosopher Alfred Whitehead has been one of the most important critics of modern science. His *Science and the Modern World*, published in 1925, sought to show that scientific thinking had become too narrow. Science had increased knowledge and brought technological progress, but had become devoid of any metaphysical understanding.

Whitehead believed that most scientists failed to appreciate the dynamic nature of the universe and the interconnections within it. Scientific progress would only be made once they recognised the importance of process, creativity, indefiniteness and what he called the "organic unity of a whole".

One of Whitehead's key ideas was that the basic metaphor for interpreting the world should not be a machine but an *organism*. The world should be seen as a web of interconnected events and mutual influences. Each entity was actually constituted by its relationships, every event had an essential reference to other times and places, and each occurrence in turn exerted an influence upon other occurrences.

He also argued that the world should be seen as in a process of becoming, open to transformation and not predetermined. These ideas became known as "process philosophy".

His stress on the value of viewing nature as a whole rather than as discrete "pieces", strongly influenced ecological philosophy. Whitehead hoped that as human perceptions changed, nature would no longer be treated as senseless, valueless and purposeless. There would be a new ethic of interdependence.

The school of "process theology" was been developed around Whitehead's philosophy, by scholars such as John Cobb. Process theology attempts to bridge the gap between science and religion by questioning the remote deistic understanding of God and the secularism of modern science.

Schumacher

A trenchant criticism of modern industrialism was made in the early 1970s by economist and Roman Catholic E.F. Schumacher.

Schumacher observed that abuse of the Earth arose out of materialism and, specifically, the deliberate cultivation and expansion of "needs", which led to greed and envy. He criticised the prevailing notion of progress and the fact that production was determined by impersonal forces rather than an assessment of genuine need.

Schumacher was especially critical of the indiscriminate application of technology, such as nuclear power, which he believed posed an unprecedented threat to the environment.

He also attacked "giantism", the use of large scale technology when small scale alternatives were available. This central belief was encapsulated in the title of his most widely read book, *Small is Beautiful*.

Schumacher attributed much of the blame for society's problems to the separation of science and values. He argued that scientific methods were wrongly applied to other disciplines, such as economics. Moreover, contemporary values were based on the philosophies of positivism and reductionism which ultimately treated people as accidental arrangements of atoms.

Porritt

The most influential contemporary exponent of green philosophy is former Green Party activist and *Friends of the Earth* Director Jonathon Porritt. His main book, *Seeing Green*, contrasts a world view based on ecology with the dominant prevailing world view of industrialism, in which industry is the most powerful force shaping society.

Porritt outlines a set of "minimum criteria for being green", an attempt to identify attitudes and beliefs which distinguish the Green philosophy from other expressions of environmentalism. These include a reverence for the earth, a rejection of materialism and the "rat race of economic growth", opposition to nuclear weapons and nuclear energy, the need for significant limits on population, and support for participatory democracy.

"Modern man has built a system of production that ravishes nature and a type of society that mutilates man... The development of production and the acquisition of wealth have thus become the highest goals of the modern world... "
E.F. Schumacher, *Small is Beautiful*

"The logic of ecology stands in direct opposition to the logic of industrialism; for it is clear that in the very process of 'succeeding', industry cannot help but destroy its own material base."
Jonathon Porritt, *Seeing Green*

GREEN THINKING

It is said by politicians that "we're all environmentalists now." And in the light of what we now know about environmental damage, who could seriously oppose some measures to protect the environment?

But the term "Green" has rather different connotations. These are associated especially with Green politics. So what does "being Green" imply?

There are five basic characteristics of Green philosophy. Here they are, with a brief Christian perspective.

Green philosophy is biocentric.

The focus of attention of green philosophy is the entire biosphere, all living things, rather than humankind alone. It is thus "biocentric" rather than "anthropocentric".

> **"The belief that we are 'apart from' the rest of creation is an intrinsic feature of the dominant world order, a man-centred or anthropocentric philosophy. Ecologists argue that this ultimately destructive belief must be rooted out and replaced with a life-centred or biocentric philosophy."** (Jonathon Porritt, *Seeing Green*)

"The values of the Greens, their commitment to justice and liberty, cannot be adequately anchored in ecology" (Martin Ryle, *Ecology and Socialism*). Do you agree? Why?

There is an obvious sense in which we *can* only view the world through human eyes. And our bond to other human beings is stronger than to other species. We may therefore want to make a clear distinction between human beings and other species. But the relatedness of all species is fundamental to Green philosophy.

Despite what some critics say, Christianity is not inherently anthropocentric. It is true that in the past, a common error has been to focus entirely on a Christian's personal relationship with Christ and to disregard the rest of creation. But a Christian world view should be directed towards how we see the relationship of Christ to the *whole* creation – in a sense it should be Christocentric *and* biocentric.

Green philosophy adopts a holistic methodology.

The philosophy of holism is summed up in the phrase: "The whole is more than the sum of the parts." It is based on a belief that different aspects of life are best understood as part of a whole. We will consider holism in depth from a Christian perspective in Unit 6.

Holism stands in contrast to reductionism (see page 19). It may be theoretically possible to base an ecological philosophy on reductionism, but it is an unlikely combination. Reductionist scientists tend to be disinterested in multidisciplinary study and thus unattracted to the wider questions of philosophy.

Green philosophy regards sustainable development as imperative.

Sustainable development aims to leave the natural environment in such a state that future generations will be able to derive from it the same level of well-being as the present generation.

Thus the motivation for human activity is not just our own survival and well-being but the need to provide for future generations. As such, it is concerned with justice across the generations, or "inter-generational equity".

"We do not inherit the Earth from our ancestors, we borrow it from our children."

As Christians we believe that God exists beyond our concept of time and is aware of all generations. The Bible warns that future generations will be punished for the sins of the present generation (Ex 20:5).

Green philosophy advocates decentralism.

Schumacher popularised the virtue of small-scale activity, arguing that all human activity should be on an appropriate scale. Decisions are best taken at the "grass roots" level rather than by remote hierarchies. Green philosophy thus embraces the principle of "subsidiarity".

"While many theoreticians - who may not be too closely in touch with real life - are still engaging in the idolatry of large size, with practical people in the actual world there is a tremendous longing and striving to profit, if at all possible, from the convenience, humanity, and manageability of smallness." (E.F. Schumacher, *Small is Beautiful*)

Christian teaching has traditionally stressed the importance of personal and community responsibility. The subsidiarity principle has its roots in Catholic teaching. The Israelites considered themselves to be a community with particular responsibilities towards each other - for example when selling land or lending money (Lev 25:25, Lev 35-37).

Green philosophy is unequivocal in radicalism.

Many adherents of Green philosophy believe that thoroughgoing political reform is needed. According to its supporters, Green politics offers a "visionary and fundamentalist challenge" to the prevailing economic and political world order.

"Tackling pollution, acid rain, famine in Africa, the annihilation of the tropical rainforests, nuclear poisoning, the destruction of the ozone layer and all the other environmental crises which face us is going to require solutions a good deal more radical than a spot of reformist tinkering with the self-same industrial system that got us into this mess in the first place." (Jonathon Porritt and David Winner, *The Coming of the Greens*)

Such thinking resonates with the understanding that Christians are to aspire to high ideals, should reject materialism, and ought not to conform with the pattern of this world (Matt 5:48, 6:24, Rom 12:2).

Each of these elements express concerns that are reflected in Christianity. Green politics can be an expression of Christian faith, even though it is often based on other religious beliefs.

TECHNOLOGY AGAINST NATURE?

What are the key distinctions in the thinking of environmentalists? On pages 56-59 we consider the spectrum of different beliefs.

Many people see themselves as concerned for the environment, but are not sympathetic to the ideas or the culture of the Green movement. There are differences amongst environmentalists, and different ways of pursuing a solution to our current ecological problems.

An important model for understanding different attempts to solve environmental problems has been developed by Tim O'Riordan in *Environmentalism*. O'Riordan argues that the search for solutions centres either around ecology or around technology. He identifies these two "modes", *ecocentrism* and *technocentrism*, which he regards as alternative world views or "life perspectives".

Ecocentrism

Underlying the ecocentric mode is an assumption that a natural order exists, and that all things operate according to the laws of nature. Nature is intrinsically important and contains its own "purpose". A delicate and perfect balance is maintained in nature – until the point at which humanity enters the picture and upsets that balance.

Ecocentrists believe that a fundamental change in people's attitudes is needed if environmental problems are to be overcome. They believe we need to adopt a more humble and humane approach to other species, live in harmony with ecological processes, and develop a sense of empathy with nature.

There is a suggestion that natural law should guide moral behaviour. People who are responsive and sympathetic to the laws of nature are considered more likely to become aware of their obligations to others and to sustain the life-supporting processes of the natural world.

Ecocentrism

- preaches the virtues of reverence, humility, responsibility and care
- argues for low impact technology (but is not anti-technological)
- decries bigness and impersonality in all forms (but especially in the city)
- demands a code of behaviour that seeks permanence and stability based upon the ecological principles of diversity and homeostasis

Critics of ecocentrism question whether a "biocentric ethic" is really possible. If values relating to nature originate from the human mind, are they not by definition anthropocentric? Are we not inevitably more concerned about our species than about others? Does nature mourn extinct or damaged species? Doesn't nature's value depend, at least in part, upon its potential usefulness to humankind?

Technocentrism

Underlying the technocentric mode, which has been dominant in the industrial era, is a belief that the natural environment is essentially "neutral". People are entitled to use it freely and to adapt and exploit it according to their desires.

Technocentrists tend to equate progress with continuous scientific and technological development. They have confidence in the capacity of experts to understand and control events, analyse problems, and overcome any obstacles by sound management. They tend to be deferential and favour hierarchical structures in society.

Technocentrism is identified by

- **rationality**, the "objective" appraisal of means to achieve given goals
- **managerial efficiency**, the application of organisational and productive techniques that produce the most for the least effort
- **optimism and faith** in people's ability to understand and control physical, biological and social processes for the benefit of present and future generations

Critics of technocentrism point to the historic failure of responses based on new or more powerful technology to overcome environmental problems. Don't new technological developments such as genetic engineering raise as many problems as they solve? Didn't Chernobyl show how dangerous it is to place substantial power over nature in the hands of scientists?

A matter of inclination?

There is in reality a spectrum of environmental concern between the ecocentric and technocentric modes. People merely *incline* towards one or the other.

But O'Riordan defines much of the spectrum as "accommodators": people who appreciate that the technocentric perspective is no longer credible or appropriate, but want to see modest change rather than radical new thinking or reform.

How might an ecocentrist and a technocentrist differ in their explanation of the cause of global warming? What solutions would you expect each to propose?

RADICAL GREEN REMEDIES

Among those who are essentially ecocentric, there is a second division of perspectives between two schools of thought, *deep ecology* and *social ecology*.

1. Deep Green

Deep ecology represents an attempt to develop a comprehensive world view based on ecology. It dismisses the scientific approach to ecology as inadequate. It is also explicitly concerned with asking religious questions and with exploring the development of an "ecological consciousness".

Deep ecology is based on the work of Norwegian philosopher Arne Naess, who in turn was influenced by Aldo Leopold. Naess developed his ideas in the early 1970s, but they became better known when popularised by American writers Bill Devall and George Sessions in the mid 1980s.

Naess based deep ecology on two "ultimate norms", *self-realisation* and *biocentric equality*. They are "ultimate" or absolute in the sense of not being derived from other principles.

Me, you and the rabbit

The principle of *self-realisation* requires that people stop seeing themselves as isolated, competing egos. Instead they should seek to identify with all other beings, human and otherwise, by rejecting contemporary assumptions and values, and by meditating in order to nurture an ecological consciousness.

The central intuition of deep ecology is there is no essential or "ontological" division in creation between the human species and the rest of the created order.

Naess considered deep ecology to be a world view which could be applied to any religious tradition. A Christian might see no problem with the idea that human beings are enriched by identification with nature. The self-realisation norm, however, goes further. The ultimate aim is the realisation of "self in Self", where "Self" stands for organic wholeness. In other words, the goal is identification with all living matter. This is indeed a world view, but one which resonates better with pantheistic monism than with Christianity.

More equal than others?

The principle of *biocentric equality* maintains that all organisms – indeed all entities – are of equal intrinsic worth. They all have the right to live, the right to procreate and develop, and the right to come to their own "self-realisation" as part of the great "Self-realisation" of the cosmos.

The principle has been challenged on several grounds. Firstly, higher levels of activity in organisms influence evolutionary history to a degree that lower levels do not. There are distinctions which are intrinsic to the natural order. Warwick Fox appreciated that the only universe in which everything was of equal value would be a dead universe.

On a practical level, the idea that all life is of equal value is problematic. Most people believe instinctively that species differ in value. Faced with the options of pulling back a cat or a child from an approaching car, people are inclined to protect the child.

Even Naess has recognised the practical limitations of biocentric equality. The killing of one species by another is a biological fact of life. Advocates of biocentric equality resort to modifying their ethic into one of "minimum impact" by human beings upon other species. This is vague enough not to be contentious, but takes the force out of the original formulation.

2. Green or red?

Social ecology is an explicitly *political* philosophy. It asserts that environmental problems have their roots in the social order, and will only be overcome through radical social change.

Social ecology has its roots in the utopian socialist tradition of William Morris and anarchists such as Peter Kropotkin. It has been popularised in recent years by an American academic, Murray Bookchin.

Whereas deep ecology is essentially concerned with individual action, social ecology emphasises the role of society and, specifically, blames capitalism and the free market for environmental problems.

Social ecology depicts nature as egalitarian, non-hierarchical and essentially cooperative. It is underpinned by a naturalist philosophy which proposes that human behaviour should reflect the order which is seen in the natural world. Bookchin concludes that human nature would best flourish in small-scale, decentralised, federated, non-hierarchical communes.

The historical dimension is important to social ecology. Bookchin writes that human beings have developed a unique social world distinct from the natural world, with hierarchies, classes, cities and states. "As both worlds interact with each other through the highly complex phases of evolution, it has become as important to speak of a social ecology as to speak of a natural ecology." (Murray Bookchin, *The Ecology of Freedom*)

Social ecology is disinterested in spirituality or religion. Bookchin's view of ecology is "avowedly rational" and he "looks to evolution and biosphere, not to deities in the sky or under the earth."

"Deep ecology... has virtually no real sense that our ecological problems have their ultimate roots in society and in social problems. It preaches a gospel of a kind of original sin that accurses a vague species called humanity, as though people of colour are equatable with whites, women with men, the Third World with the First, the poor with the rich, and the exploited with the exploiters."
Murray Bookchin in Porritt and Winner, *The Coming of the Greens*

JAINISM

One religious tradition which takes biocentric equality very seriously is Jainism, an offshoot of Hinduism. Jains try not to harm any sentient being. Jain monks carry a hand brush formed of twigs to sweep the ground before them, so as to avoid stepping on any creatures. They also cover their mouths to avoid inadvertently breathing in any insects.

GOING FURTHER

Red, blue, orange, black, brown and green...

Green ideas have attracted the interest of political philosophies from all traditions, as well as forming the basis for a new political philosophy.

Socialists argue that environmental problems can only be resolved through collective action.

Conservatives believe that such problems often arise because environmental assets are not priced in the market situation.

Liberals have historically advocated social change, including environmental sustainability, while stressing the role of individuals, local authorities and international bodies more than the national state.

Anarchists dismiss the role of government and stress the importance of action by individual grass-roots activists.

Even **neo-fascists** have embraced green ideas, linking the love of the soil with devotion to the nation state.

Additional reading

Stephen Clark's *How to Think about the Earth* and Laurence Osborn's *Guardians of Creation* provide useful critiques of ideas underpinning Green philosophy, from a Christian perspective. See also chapter 4 in Tim Cooper, *Green Christianity*. Despite being a touch out of date, the most accessible exposition of the philosophy of the Green movement remains Jonathon Porritt's *Seeing Green*. A slightly more recent and broader description of the movement is Jonathon Porritt and David Winner's *The Coming of the Greens*. Henryk Skolimowski's *Eco-Philosophy* was an early influence. Different environmental perspectives are found in Timothy O'Riordan's *Environmentalism*, Bill Devall and George Sessions's *Deep Ecology* and Murray Bookchin's *The Ecology of Freedom*.

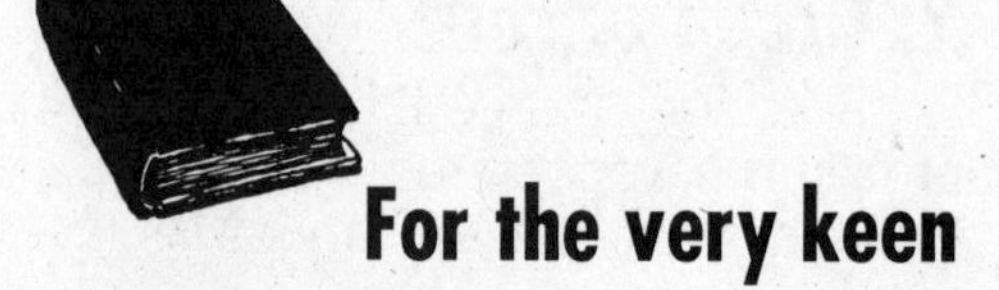

For the very keen

Jonathon Porritt, *Seeing Green*, Chapters 1, 2, 4, 8, 9, 14, 15
In the most influential Green book of the 1980s Jonathon Porritt contrasts the politics of ecology with the politics of industrialism. What elements within the Green critique of modern industrial society outlined by Porritt make the spiritual dimension to Green philosophy so imperative?

E.F. Schumacher, *Small is Beautiful*, Chapters 1-6
Schumacher explains the inability of contemporary economics to meet people's needs. What would you highlight as the major factors which lead him to issue his plea for "metaphysical reconstruction"?

Jonathon Porritt and David Winner, *The Coming of the Greens*, Chapters 1-3, 6, 8, 11 & 12
A popular examination of the contemporary influence of the Green movement. Do you accept that there has been "an extraordinary growth in green values", as a report quoted in the book suggests (p 122)? Or do you believe that the influence of the movement is relatively small and its wide scale publicity mere hype?

Donald Worster, *Nature's Economy*, Chapters 13-15
The concluding section of Worster's history of ecology. What are the sources of the division between ecologists inclined towards "pragmatic utilitarianism" and those motivated by an "organic, communal ideal"?

SUSTAINING THE EARTH

UNIT 6

SEEING THE WHOLE

CONTENTS

PURPOSE

The purpose of this Unit is to understand the implications of the essential proposition of environmentalists that we should think "holistically".

DEFINING HOLISM

It is impossible to understand the environment without thinking in terms of relationships. As biologist Barry Commoner once said, "Everything is connected to everything else."

"Holism" is a way of thinking which focuses on w**hol**e systems rather than parts. The term was first coined in the late 1920s. Reality is seen in terms of integrated wholes, the properties of which cannot be reduced to the properties of their smaller units.

The whole exhibits distinctive behaviour by virtue of its totality.

There are, of course, situations in which study of isolated parts is necessary. The task is to judge the circumstances and decide whether wider interactions may legitimately be discounted.

The World Council of Churches has in recent years adopted the phrase "integrity of creation" to describe the relationships and balances which exist in the natural world. "Integrity" in this context is understood as wholeness or unity.

Holism and science

Much scientific work has been based on a reductionist approach. People have sought to reduce things, objects or facts to the smallest indivisible components, and then reconstruct them.

Increasingly, however, scientists have found that reductionist methodologies provide inadequate explanations of reality. This is true of nuclear physics as well as ecology. Species or objects are often understood better in the context of their surroundings.

In scientific ecology, holism explains the formation of wholes by ordered groupings that are more than the sum of the parts, as in the evolution from atoms and cells to complex forms of life and mind.

"The whole is greater than the sum of its parts."
William Blake

As early as 1931 the eminent scientist J.B.S. Haldane wrote that biologists "must always keep the whole organism in view." Austrian biologist Ludwig von Bertalanffy, who developed systems theory, was another important influence in the 1930s.

Holism and theology

The history of ever-increasing specialisation culminated in the late 19th century in the virtually total separation of theology from the scientific disciplines. This was in part fuelled by the church's fear that the inherent determinism of the scientific approach would "contaminate" Christian theology.

Scientists and theologians have recently begun to reverse this process:

- **Physicists** such as Ian Barbour and John Polkinghorne have written influential studies on the compatibility of modern science and theology.

- **Theologians** such as Jurgen Moltmann have argued that this separation will not last, partly because science's earlier unquestioning faith in itself has disappeared. Eventually "theology and the sciences will arrive together at the ecological awareness of the world" (*God in Creation*).

Holism in practice

Holism is not just a theoretical concept; it has wider implications:

- In **health care** practitioners of complementary medicine treat people as whole beings. Attention is paid not merely to physiological symptoms but to people's state of mind and even their spiritual beliefs.

- In **Green politics** the interrelationship between economic and environmental objectives is increasingly recognised.

- In **religious practice** a holistic approach is leading many Christians to recognise that faith should permeate and affect the whole of life.

"Since the beginning of time our task as humans has been to harmonise the spiritual and material realms. We were intended to be mediators between God and His creation, but have been disobedient. In our failure, God, in human form, fulfils this task by uniting Himself to His creation in the closest possible way, taking the form of that which he created."

Tim Cooper, ***Green Christianity***

"We must 'give space' to all the plurality of dimensions of life. We do not do this in a 'split' way of sanctifying certain areas, making them subservient to, and vehicles for other, 'more important' dimensions, but we affirm their goodness in their own right."

Steve Shaw, ***No Splits***

THE ENEMIES OF HOLISM

Holism is a response to
- **the dominance of *reductionism* in science**
- **the powerful influence of *dualism* in Western culture.**

"One of the greatest challenges to the Christian faith today is the reductionist image of man as a complex machine whose operation can in principle be exhaustively explained by the laws of physics and chemistry."
Ian Barbour

Reductionism

Reductionism is an attempt to understand whole entities by studying and analysing their parts.

Critics argue that it is inadequate because it abstracts things from the full complexity of reality. By doing so, it offers only a partial understanding of them. Moreover, it assumes that the behaviour of a system can be explained by the laws governing its components.

This is not to say that reductionist methods are never of use. In sciences such as physics, chemistry and molecular biology, a reductionist approach may be appropriate "to discover the structure and function of each cog and bolt in nature's machinery" (Paul Ehrlich, *Nature's Machinery*). Molecular biology, for example, has provided important discoveries about heredity.

But, argues Ehrlich, reductionism is inappropriate for ecology and evolutionary biology, because these disciplines are trying to understand the "present structure and operation of the entire apparatus, as well as the history of its construction." When we want to know how the whole ecosystem works and how it comes to be the way it is, the holistic approach is more appropriate.

Dehumanising

Francis Crick was one of the scientists who discovered DNA, the chemical structure of the material that carries hereditary biological information. He once asserted that he aimed to explain all biology in terms of chemistry and physics.

The danger is that reductionism may lead to a false understanding of how the natural world operates. Is our consciousness and awareness of the world around us no more than a series of complex physical-chemical interactions in the brain? Are human beings like machines operating according to predetermined codes? Reductionism is ultimately dehumanising. It implies that there is no free will and that human behaviour is determined solely by genes and environmental influences.

Dominating

Reductionism is sometimes linked to a desire to dominate the object being studied. In studying the environment we may treat ourselves as the "subject" and thus reduce nature to an "object".

Moltmann argues that if a doctrine of creation is to be ecological we must avoid this distinction. Linking people's motives and methodologies, he suggests people often "desire to know in order to dominate... [and]... analyse and reduce in order to reconstruct." Instead we can "strive to learn a new, communicative and integrating way of thought." Our intention should be "to perceive in order to participate."

Distorting

Reductionism aims to simplify reality by discounting the significance of relationships. Ultimately it is flawed simply because everything that exists does so in relation to something else. Nothing can be properly defined apart from relationships.

A tree is more than a biological entity. It has other dimensions, among them economic, geographical, aesthetic – even political, if it is subject to a Tree Preservation Order.

Dualism

Dualism is characterised by a strict division of realities into contrasting elements: spiritual and material, mind and body, sacred and secular.

Dualistic thought has origins in the 3rd century, when the Neo-Platonists stressed the transcendence of God, and the Manicheists argued that everything sprang from two principles, good and evil, light and dark.

Rejecting dualism does not mean that no contrasts are valid. We still face choices between obedience and disobedience to God, moral rights and wrongs.

Mind and matter

The influence of Descartes, the 17th century pioneer of modern Western philosophy, has been profound (see page 18). In "Cartesian" philosophy mind and matter are separate. The mind is an immaterial, free and rational entity which inhabits and controls a machine-like body. Descartes wrote that "there is nothing included in the concept of body that belongs to the mind; and nothing in that of mind that belongs to the body."

Descartes believed that mind and matter alike were created by God. God represented a common reference point, being the source of the natural order and of the "light of reason" that enabled the human mind to recognise this order. But many scientists who have been influenced by his thinking have rejected this reference to God.

This division of mind and matter has had a major impact on Western society. It goes some way towards explaining why mental (white collar) work has had a higher status than manual (blue collar) work. It also lies behind the failure of modern medicine to take the psychological dimension to health seriously until relatively recently.

Body and soul

Dualism has had an important – and unfortunate – influence on Western theology. The spiritual world of the soul has often been contrasted with the material world of bodies. The human mind has been associated with the soul and so held in high esteem. Thus human beings were regarded as separate from the rest of nature because they possessed a "rational soul" which other species lacked. The human body – and matter generally – were considered to have no lasting consequence.

By contrast, Eastern Orthodoxy, rooted in the teachings of the early Greek Fathers, emerged in a dualistic culture but developed a theological integration of the spiritual and the material. According to its teaching, there is in human beings a permanent and essential unity between body and soul which is only temporarily broken at death. Relationships in creation continue eternally: "The body… is an integral part of human personhood. The separation of body and soul at death is unnatural, something contrary to God's original plan…[and]… only temporary." (Kallistos Ware, *The Orthodox Way*).

Dualism in the Bible?

Does the Bible and, specifically the gospel of John, teach the separation of the spiritual and material?

Whereas Matthew, Mark and Luke contrast the present age with the age to come, John compares the world "above" with life on Earth. This may encourage "otherworldliness".

Elsewhere in John's gospel, however, there are passages which are very positive towards the natural world. In chapter 1 the description of the Word being made "flesh" appears to be a deliberate rebuttal of the dualism of the Gnostics.

"Christianity is the most materialistic of all great religions… Christianity, based as it is on the Incarnation, regards matter as destined to be the vehicle and instrument of spirit, and spirit as fully actual so far as it controls and directs matter."

William Temple, *Readings in St John's Gospel*

THINK!

How might a dualistic framework of thought affect how a Christian spends his or her time and views activities outside the church? Think of any advantages and disadvantages of only joining organisations which operate from an explicitly Christian basis.

ALL IS ONE?

"Separateness is the illusion. One and many are the same."
Goethe

If dualism is rejected, what structure of reality *would* fit with holistic, ecological philosophy?

Monism

One option is monism. This is the belief that all reality is of one kind, and all forms of being may ultimately be referred to one category. Monism may take the form of

- **idealism**, in which thoughts and ideas are the basis of reality
- **materialism**, which denies the independent existence of spirit

Prominent monist thinkers include the 17th century philosopher de Spinoza and the poet Goethe. De Spinoza saw no boundary between God and creation, and viewed the world as independent, self-sufficient and eternal. Goethe wrote, "Matter cannot exist and be operative without spirit, nor spirit without matter."

Monism attracted new interest at the turn of the century through the work of German zoologist Ernst Haeckel, who first coined the term "ecology". He wrote that monism "recognises one sole substance in the universe, which is at once 'God and nature'; body and spirit (or matter and energy) it holds to be inseparable" (*The Riddle of the Universe*).

Pantheism

Philosophical ideas are often closely linked to particular religious beliefs. Haeckel concluded that the "God of dualism leads necessarily to Theism, while the God of the monist leads to pantheism."

In pantheism God is identified with the whole universe. He is the one, all-embracing, infinite, ultimate reality.

Pantheism contrasts with Christian belief in a God who retains a distinctiveness from the world, a God both immanent and transcendent, present and beyond. As C.S. Lewis observed, God and the world must be distinguished because what makes and what is made must be two and not one.

In Christianity God's Spirit penetrates the world but God Himself is not merged into it. He creates the world and enters into it, but He does not become part of it. He is sovereign and has not limited His ability and freedom to act upon it.

The intention of monism may be to avoid reductionism and acknowledge the value of the whole. However, from a Christian perspective, it distorts the true images of nature, humankind and God by ignoring their essential differences.

NO MORE THAN GRASS

In *Pollution and the Death of Man* Francis Schaeffer criticised pantheism on the basis that it "gives no meaning to any particulars" and "if the particulars have no meaning, then nature has no meaning, including the particular of man."

Pantheism, he wrote, provides an explanation for unity, but not for diversity. Instead of elevating nature, it reduces humankind to "no more than grass".

One possible outcome of pantheism is a romantic anthropomorphism, the projection of human feelings into nature.

Another is a skewed value system as in India, where "rats and cows are allowed to eat up food that man needs."

Panentheism

A more acceptable alternative to dualism for Christians may be panentheism. In panentheism God is not "above" nature. Everything takes place *within* God and He is *in* all things (see Acts 17:28). God thus interacts reciprocally with the world, sharing its experiences and destiny, and is Himself influenced by events.

Look back to page 25 for our previous discussion of panentheism, and to page 53 for the origin of process theology.

According to Jurgen Moltmann, God does not merely make, preserve, maintain and perfect the world, a relationship which Moltmann describes as "one-sided". God is indwelling, sympathizing, participating, accompanying, enduring, delighting and glorifying, in relationships of "mutuality".

But many Christians object to process theology because it threatens God's sovereignty – His transcendence, freedom and independence. As God persuades rather than compels, His power to act is limited. While He is absolved from responsibility for evil, this is at the expense of His ability to overcome it.

Are you convinced by these attempts to see all of reality as essentially one? Is it possible to look at the world "holistically" from a Christian point of view, while avoiding both monism and dualism?

"To realise one's oneness with the cosmos is to pass beyond personality" (James Sire). What does the Bible teach concerning self-consciousness? Is there any conflict in Christian thinking between self-sacrifice and self-fulfilment? (See Matt 19:19, Mark 8:34-35, Phil 2:3)

Pluralism?

Is there, then, an alternative philosophy for Christians who reject dualism and are uneasy about monism because of its direct route to pantheism? Might pluralism help?

Pluralism recognises a multitude of different forms of being, and teaches that there is no absolute or total unity throughout all things. Unity is a partial, rather than absolute, truth.

One example of pluralism is its use by Dutch Christian philosopher Herman Dooyeweerd. He distinguished fifteen "modes" of being, such as the spatial, physical, biotic, lingual, social, economic and juridical. Each reflects a different aspect of human experience.

Thus when looking at a tree it is not enough to identify whether it is "material", spiritual", or both. A tree can be explained in a multitude of different ways according to which "mode" is used by the observer.

Some blind men were trying to describe an elephant from what they could feel. Each of them described it differently, as...

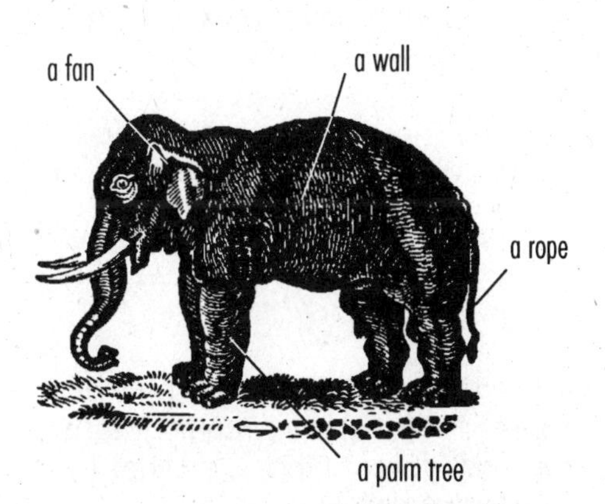

Pluralism is also used in a secular context to promote the value of diversity, such as in the defence of equal opportunities for ethnic minorities.

A weakness of pluralism from a Christian perspective is that it shies away from any consideration of absolute truth. Thus in multi-cultural education, all religious faiths tend to be treated as equally valid.

HOLISTIC THEOLOGY

What theological models are available to Christians who want to think holistically?

A "theology of ecology" would be centred upon God as revealed in Jesus Christ, and concerned with the structure and function of the *whole* creation. It would necessarily be holistic, characterised by a recognition of our intrinsic interdependence with all aspects of the natural world.

Such a theology will take time to evolve, but is already emerging in books such as Moltmann's *God in Creation* (subtitled "an ecological doctrine of creation").

A theology of ecology may be used in two ways.

- ☛ **Theology can be applied to ecology.** We can, for example, make assumptions about how God works as we study the environment.
- ☛ **An ecological framework can be used in theological study.** We can take ideas and arguments used by environmentalists, the models, language and philosophy of ecology, and consider what they imply for our understanding of God.

Several theological traditions provide the historical context for the emerging theology of ecology:

Natural theology

In natural theology, the orderliness and intelligence of nature is regarded as evidence of the existence of God.

From the 19th century onwards, Darwinism challenged natural theology with the claim that the appearance of design in nature merely reflected a process of adaptation through random variation and natural selection. Other critics have suggested that organisms might in themselves contain organising principles, thus discounting any need for an external deity to explain the ordered nature of the universe.

Even so, the evidence of an intelligent Designer has proved resilient and persuasive to many Christians. Nature as the source of "wonder" still leads people to belief in God (see page 34).

A theology of nature

In the Protestant tradition greater emphasis has been put on the historical revelation of God recorded in the Scriptures. Moltmann's primary interest is "not what nature can contribute to our knowledge of God, but what the concept of God contributes to our knowledge of nature."

Here a theology of nature is concerned with understanding the relation of God and humankind to the natural environment. Such a theology provides the basis for a Christian interpretation of environmental ethics.

What of the effect of our industrial activities upon our surroundings – the creation of the "secular city"? In order to take account of the "built" environment as well as the natural environment, perhaps it is more appropriate to talk of a "theology of the environment".

A theology of creation

A theology of creation is concerned with the creative acts of God and the unfolding of creation.

The distinction between "nature" and "creation" is important. Nature is only the visible aspect to creation. The concept of creation goes beyond that of nature, embracing not merely the environment outside of us, but also ourselves as conscious subjective beings.

Some theologians use the term "theology of creation" (rather than theology of *nature*) because of the risk of separating humankind from nature and then objectifying nature. They argue that once God's creation is understood as mere "nature", it is easier to justify its exploitation.

Creationism is a fundamentalist school of thought in which Genesis is interpreted literally and in strict contrast to Darwinism. In creationism, God's activity in "creation" tends to be understood in a narrow sense, as happening only at the beginning of time rather than as a continual process.

Creation-centred spirituality

A very different approach is taken by proponents of creation-centred spirituality, using the writings of Matthew Fox and Thomas Berry.

According to Fox, much of the blame for environmental abuse, social oppression and a fear of passion lies with the fall/redemption tradition which originated with Augustine. Fox highlights the words of Thomas a Kempis: "Every time I go into creation, I withdraw from God."

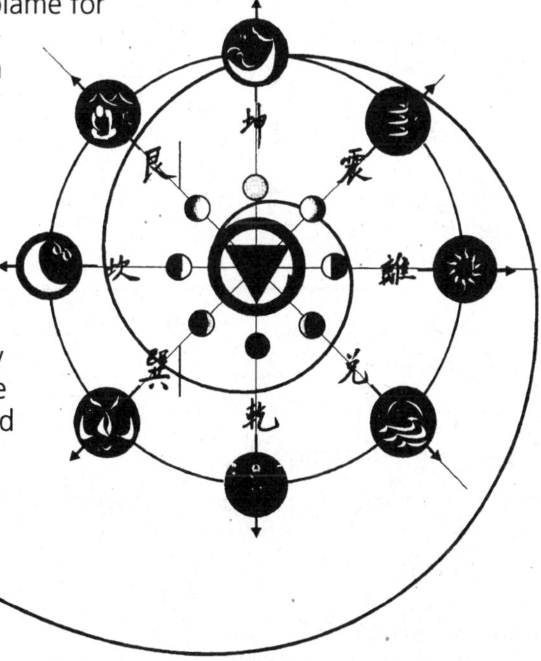

Creation-centred spirituality shifts the theological focus away from original sin, the fall and the human need for redemption, and onto creation and our need to celebrate life and creativity.

Advocates of creation-centred spirituality claim that it draws on a long established tradition which has been suppressed and only kept alive through artists, poets and mystics. Critics point to its unorthodox elements and dubious interpretations of past theologians. Fox was forced out of the Roman Catholic Church in which he had been a Dominican priest.

THE VALUE OF ALL LIFE

From a holistic perspective all forms of life are significant because all life is connected. All life has value.

Augustine wrote that evil is not a substance. "All nature's substances are good, because they exist and have their own mode and kind of being, and, in their fashion, a peace and harmony among themselves." When God created the Earth, he blessed it in its entirety.

But we undervalue the Earth. An example is our willingness to cause widespread environmental destruction. Jonathan Schell argued that the presence of nuclear weapons signifies a belief that life is dispensable or valueless (*The Fate of the Earth*).

While God has blessed creation in its entirety, He has granted humankind a degree of freedom to use it. Our attitudes towards the Earth and our activities upon it signify how much we value each part of it. Consciously or otherwise, we make an evaluation and take greatest care of those parts which we value highly. We discriminate in our treatment of other people and other species.

Different continents

Most environmental issues have a global dimension. But are people in different countries valued equally?

Air pollution does not stop at national boundaries. Fossil fuels and raw materials are often obtained from global markets. Internationally co-ordinated measures are necessary for a comprehensive response to environmental problems, but these invariably raise issues of global justice.

Consider global warming. If increases in the Earth's temperature are not to threaten major damage, the emission of greenhouse gases such as carbon dioxide needs to be reduced. What does this mean for rich industrialised countries and poor countries? Arguably, if we value people's lives equally, it should be those who are already relatively rich who should cut their consumption and bear the cost of pollution abatement equipment.

Different generations

Environmentalists often quote the saying: "We do not inherit the Earth from our parents, we borrow it from our children." But do we live as if we value the wellbeing of future generations as highly as our own?

Natural resources such as fossil fuels, metals and minerals are in finite supply. If we were properly concerned about future generations, we would adopt a deliberate policy of restraint, in order to make them last longer. We would increase energy efficiency, use renewable energy resources, and recycle metals and minerals.

The value of relations

If our approach to Christianity is holistic, we will acknowledge and value the interconnections within the created order. The meaning and purpose of life cannot be adequately understood except in relation to the Creator and the rest of His creation.

All connections within creation are of fundamental importance:

- Alienation from God leads to spiritual impoverishment and destruction.
- Broken relationships between people result in social disintegration.
- Disregarding our links with nature is the source of environmental damage.

We are able to restore these links. But we will need to develop our awareness of God's interaction with His creation. We will have to empower local communities to work together to overcome local economic and environmental problems. And we will take more care of the natural environment, in recognition that we depend upon its life support systems.

THE CREATIVE TRINITY

God the Father creates through the Son and the Holy Spirit. The act of creation is "a corporate act of the three persons of the trinity" (Paulos Mar Gregorios).

Western Christianity has in the past identified only God the Father with the "first cause", the source of creation. But what of Christ and the Holy Spirit?

Creating in the Spirit

"Creation in the Spirit" is a phrase used by Moltmann to describe the fact that God always creates through and in the power of His Spirit. God's Spirit is in all created beings, because everything that exists is able to do so only through the Spirit's unceasing flow into creation (Ps 104). "Nothing in the world exists, lives and moves of itself." God's Spirit is "the sustaining foundation" of everything and brings to life a "community" or "fellowship" of creation. Through His Spirit all created things communicate with one another and with God, each in its own way.

Christ and creation

Old Testament scholar Bernhard Anderson writes of the need to understand creation in the light of God's action in Christ ("Christologically"). In Christ God has restored the human pattern intended at the original creation.

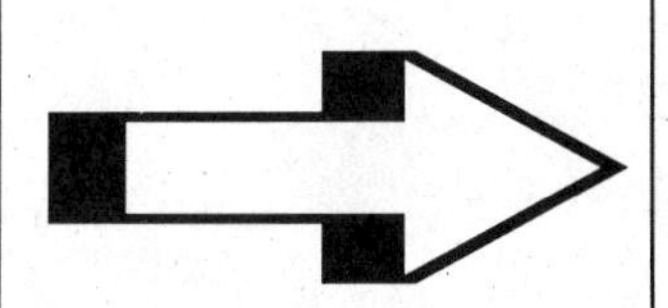

GOING FURTHER

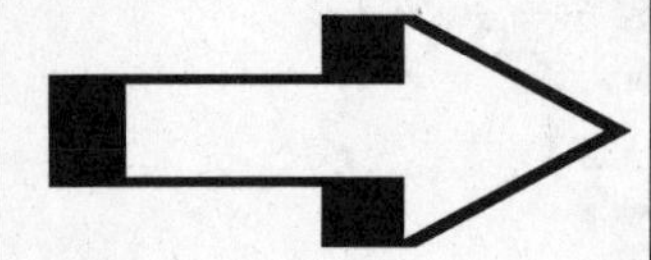

The epistles portray Christ as the revelation of God's purpose and this undergirds the whole creation. Christ comes as the bearer of the meaning of history and creation, as Creator and Redeemer.

Paulos Mar Gregorios similarly suggests that we should no longer see Christ as abstract or purely spiritual, "somehow totally distinct from the created order." Even now Christ shares his being with the whole created order. "He took matter into himself, so matter is not alien to him now."

Additional reading

The chapter on "The Value of Life" in Tim Cooper's *Green Christianity* expands some of the areas covered in this Unit, as does Paulos Mar Gregorios's thought-provoking chapter "New Testament Foundations for Understanding the Creation" in Wesley Granberg-Michaelson's *Tending the Garden*. *Contours of a World View* by Arthur Holmes contains two chapters on theological and philosophical approaches to God and creation. Steve Shaw's *No Splits* is brief and accessible. As well as providing a detailed study of world views Richard Walsh and Brian Middleton's *The Transforming Vision* contains a useful critique of dualism. Patrick Pietroni's *Holistic Living* is informative (though not explicitly Christian). There is a journal, *Eco-theology*, which contain the latest theological ideas relating to ecology.

For the very keen

Steve Shaw, *No Splits*
In this critique of dualistic thought Steve Shaw argues that only by linking belief and behaviour in all areas of life can the Christian faith come alive. Is the Christian faith truly applicable to all spheres of life? What difference might being a Christian make to how a person approaches a new job opportunity, dresses, plays a game of tennis, or decides what food to purchase? Why?

James W Sire, *The Universe Next Door*, Chapters 1, 2, & 7
An important systematic study of major 'world views'. Compare the key propositions of Christian theism and eastern pantheistic monism outlined by the author, and consider which appears more likely to lead to holistic thought.

Brian Walsh and Richard Middleton, *The Transforming Vision*, Chapters 6, 7, 10, 11 & 12
In this study the authors argue that a biblical world view is comprehensive and affects the whole of life. How does their critique of dualism expose the dangers of teaching ecology as a science?

Arthur Holmes, *Contours of a World View*, Chapters 6, 7 & 11
A rigorous attempt to develop a world view with distinctively Christian presuppositions. Explain why monism has a distorting effect on how we see reality, and describe how a biblical understanding of relational differences helps to define the parameters and possibilities of responsible human behaviour.

Ian G Barbour, *Issues in Science and Religion*, Chapter 11
A fascinating systematic study of the relationship between science and theology. What are the key objections to dualist and reductionist methods in understanding human beings? How might a "metaphysics of levels" contribute to a holistic understanding which takes biblical and scientific insights into account?

SUSTAINING THE EARTH

UNIT 7

PARTNERSHIP WITH IDOLATRY?

CONTENTS

PURPOSE

The purpose of this Unit is to consider whether environmentalists are making religious claims which are incompatible with Christianity, and, if so, how we can work alongside them in preserving the world.

WORKING WITH ENVIRONMENTALISTS

Journalists have often caricatured environmentalists as young, scruffy, inclined towards vegetarianism, woolly minded, and unrealistic about the "real world". Even if there was ever truth in this image, much has changed since the upsurge in concern about environmental issues in the late 1980s.

The scale and diversity of the environmental movement is reflected in support from people of all ages, backgrounds and beliefs. People become actively involved in environmental campaigns for many reasons:

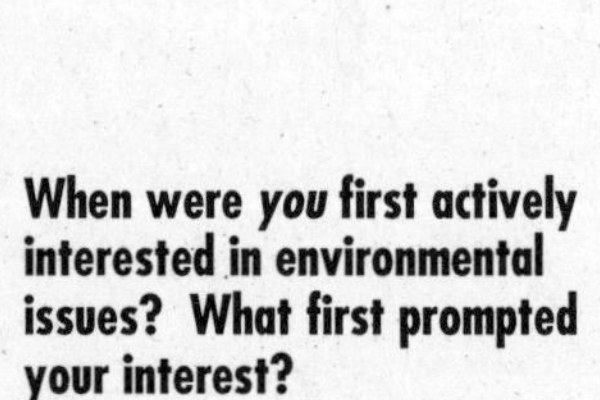

When were *you* first actively interested in environmental issues? What first prompted your interest?

- **NIMBYs** – the "Not In My Back Yard" environmentalists who protest against a nearby development which would affect them personally
- **Parents** – those whose concern about the future has increased because of parenthood and their concern for their children
- **Political idealists** – people who are attracted to the vision of a better world set out in political ideologies
- **Romantics** – those who have a positive image of the environment of past eras
- **Spiritual seekers** – people who have made a religious commitment and reject materialism, being sceptical of finding happiness by acquiring wealth

It is important that Christians who intend to become actively involved in environmental projects should not hold preconceived ideas about the kinds of people environmentalists are. We need to accept them as we find them.

Christians will want to understand the motivation which inspires others to protect the environment. Some environmentalists may not have thought through their reasons and are simply seeking to improve the quality of life. Others will be acting out of clearly defined ideological beliefs.

A bunch of pagans?

A right wing "think tank", the Institute for Economic Affairs, has argued that many environmental activists have pagan or pantheistic beliefs. In reality, though, environmentalists have a wide range of religious beliefs.

Most people are "religious" in the sense that they search for firm beliefs and need to make commitments. Those who are not satisfied with the Christian faith look for absolutes elsewhere.

The different beliefs described in this Unit can be treated either as insights or as idols. Some people will regard the statements below as conditional and tentative. But in the absence of any Christian commitment, people may turn them into credal statements – absolute truths which demand unquestioning commitment. The principles become, in effect, idols, taking the place of obedience to God.

1. Life must continue

Total commitment to the continuation of life on this Earth represents an *idol of sustainability*, and makes a religion out of evolution. In contrast Christianity talks of the new creation in which Christians will have new bodies and the Earth will be radically transformed (1 Cor 15:35-36, 2 Pet 3.10-11).

2. All life is one

Belief that all life is one represents an *idol of unity*, the religion of pantheistic monism. In the New Age movement people believe that all reality can be reduced to one category, which may be equated with God. Our selves and our environment are regarded as the outward expression of the divine reality. This is at variance with the Christian belief that our Creator God is not wholly bound by the creation. He transcends it and is able to act upon it.

3. The planet is a self-regulating organism

This idea has attracted much interest in recent years. The *idol of the Earth mother* (or Gaia) is also seen in the modern revival of paganism and often promoted in eco-feminist literature. Worship of deities in nature was a sin frequently committed by the Israelites and strongly condemned by the prophets and the apostle Paul (Deut 12:2-3, Jer 10:1-11, Rom 1:21-3).

4. Truth is invariably found through science

Then there is the *idol of scientific ecology*, in which faith is placed in the certainty of scientific evidence. Science becomes scientism, a substitute religion by which all other claims to truth are judged. When science is regarded in this way as the highest source of truth, it is brought into conflict with Christianity, which recognises other sources of revelation and knowledge.

5. All life is of equal value

Finally, the interconnectedness of life has led some people to conclude that all life must be of equal value. This is the *idol of biocentric equality*, seen in deep ecology. Christianity, in contrast, holds that human beings have a unique value to God, being made in His image (Gen 1:26-27). See further page 83.

"Elementary ecology leads straight to elementary Buddhism."
Aldous Huxley

ANYTHING GOES?

Many people argue that even if one religion is uniquely true and positive towards nature, it will be impossible to convert everyone to it before environmental problems reach crisis point. Thus, it is said, the religious "strategy" of environmentalism should be to encourage followers of all religions to take care of the environment. This approach has been promoted by, among others, the World Wide Fund for Nature.

According to some environmentalists, all religions contain a positive view of nature, even if this has sometimes been suppressed.

LIFE MUST CONTINUE!

The present age is the first in which it has been possible to conceive of the destruction of the whole creation. Unlike our ancestors, we no longer assume that life on Earth will inevitably continue. So an important element in ecological thought is that the continuation of life is imperative.

Is that all?

Many environmentalists seek to improve the quality of life in this world – believing that there will be no other. They may not have a coherent vision of their ultimate goal, but they are motivated by a desire to create a better world for future generations.

Something to make the future appear more attractive is often felt to be needed. Evolution is sometimes portrayed as a dreary process of chance and necessity. Yet many people want a sense that the world is "getting better" – that the process of change represents progress. They want to see that new values and enhanced states of well-being are in prospect.

Evolving to perfection?

Henryk Skolimowski has urged people to recognize and cherish the *process* which has created the world as we know it – evolution itself. This is to be the source of our confidence in a future for us and our world. "As I see it we are part of the evolutionary unfolding, and in realizing evolution, we are actualizing our own potential."

"I owe an allegiance to the planet that has made me possible, and to all the life on that planet, whether friendly or not. I also owe an allegiance to the 31 billion years of life that made it possible for me to be here, and all the rest of you too."
David Brower

Earlier in the 20th century biologist Julian Huxley was a leading advocate of this kind of evolution-centred religious commitment. He saw no place for God, and placed his faith in the capacity of humankind to evolve through learning from the past. He believed that ethical norms could be found by observing evolutionary change.

Other evolutionary philosophers have overtly linked evolution and spirituality. The French neo-Romantic Henri Bergson saw evidence of a creative force within nature, the *elan vital* (vital impulse), guiding the universe to higher forms. His contemporary, Samuel Alexander, believed in an emergent deity, a God-ideal not yet realised. He sought through this to explain apparently purposeful behaviour in the universe, without a belief in external divine determination.

The Awakening Earth

More recently Peter Russell has speculated about an evolution of human consciousness. Russell imagines the biosphere as a unified living system with humankind acting as the nerve cells of an awakening "global brain". He points to a general trend towards greater complexity – increasing diversity, organisation and connectivity - and argues that when certain levels of complexity are reached, new levels of evolution emerge.

Ultimately, he argues, the world will become a conscious, thinking, perceiving "being", functioning at a new evolutionary level with faculties beyond human imagination. We are currently on the threshold of a major evolutionary transition in which humanity will be integrated into the rest of creation – to become a "social super-organism". This newly raised consciousness is not predetermined, however, but will come about only if we change how we perceive ourselves in relation to the world – experiencing an "inner evolution". If we do not, we will act as a "planetary cancer".

In Russell's thesis, the evolutionary process is internalised within humanity. The universe evolves through us. "The urge that many people feel to grow and develop inwardly is nothing less than the force of evolution manifesting within our own consciousness… Inner, conscious evolution is the particular phase of evolution that we, in this little corner of the universe, are currently passing through" (*The Awakening Earth*). The idea of a "thinking universe" is also seen in the Gaia hypothesis (see page 81).

Evolutionary Christianity?

Many Christians may find such ideas difficult to accept. However some aspects of evolutionary thought have been accepted by Christians:

☛ Catholic priest **Pierre Teilhard de Chardin** held a vision of a process in which the universe evolves with ever-increasing complexity and consciousness towards an "omega point", a climax when all is consummated in Christ.

☛ The idea of an evolving universe is also important in **process theology**. God's creation evolves over time while He changes alongside it, luring its species towards His ultimate purpose.

Such evolutionary Christianity has been criticised for its treatment of sin and suffering: it can reduce evil to a mere by-product of the process of evolution. More fundamentally, far from revealing increasing perfection in life, history reveals repeated cul-de-sacs and extinctions of whole groups of species.

The Old Testament prophets looked at the world around them and called people to obedience. As Christians we need to engage in the prophetic task of creating images of the future based on Biblical ideals and identifying how to move towards them. An image of a future "ecotopia" may be helpful in guiding us towards necessary change.

> ***"As Christians we are not concerned primarily about survival, either personal or collective."***
> Paulos Mar Gregorios

Ultimately, however, Christianity is distinctive in that it does not see the transformation from our present world to heaven as an unbroken continuum. Several Biblical passages indicate that after the second coming of Christ there is to be a break with the past, the bringing to birth of "a new heaven and a new earth" (Is 65:17, Rev 21:1).

GETTING BETTER?

Is the state of the world going to improve? Christians disagree about whether the future should be viewed with optimism or pessimism. The Bible speaks of the immediate presence of God's kingdom (e.g. Luke 17:20-1), but also foretells an era of turbulence (e.g. Matt 24).

ALL LIFE IS ONE

Ecology is fundamentally concerned with interrelationships, so it is attractive to those who believe that there is some deeper unity structured into the universe. This is one reason why ecological ideas are enthusiastically taken up by the New Age movement, which inclines towards pantheistic monism.

New Age predictions

The central conviction of the New Age movement is that we are on the threshold of a new era of harmony, as the universe moves from the Age of Pisces to the Age of Aquarius. As this new era breaks there will be sweeping changes, including a worldwide transformation in "human consciousness", a global spiritual reawakening resulting in a golden era of unity.

Although the New Age movement has been influential, it remains relatively small. There is, however, widespread acceptance of a concept often used in New Age writings – the "paradigm shift". A paradigm shift is a "profound change in the thoughts, perceptions and values that form a particular vision of reality" (Fritjof Capra, *The Turning Point*). Such thinking originated in the work of Thomas Kuhn, historian Arnold Toynbee and sociologist Pitirim Sorokin.

Many people believe that a major social transition of this kind is currently under way. This is reflected in growing scepticism towards the mechanistic view of the universe and towards associated beliefs in scientific certainty, objectivity and detachment. New thinking is superseding these ideas – which, it is argued, will lead to cultural transformation.

New Age followers espouse many environmental causes, but they do not believe that solutions will be found through parliament, technology, or the established religions – at least in their current forms. Instead, what is necessary is an appreciation of:

* the interdependence between mind, body and spirit
* the interdependence between people
* the interdependence between humankind and the rest of creation

In New Age thought, recognition of the "oneness" of all life is the most fundamental expression of spiritual awareness.

One with all

New Age followers believe that people can realise their full potential through meditation, dietary change and various other forms of self-development.

This self-development may include embracing psychotherapy, following the humanistic psychology of Abraham Maslow. Maslow suggested the possibility of personal growth or "self-actualisation" through the nurture of feelings, desires and hopes.

Transcendence is seen as the highest human need. The ultimate self-actualisation is to achieve a sense of transcendence in which someone reaches beyond themselves and "becomes one with all of reality".

One means of achieving this transcendence is through experiences of nature, especially in areas free from any permanent human presence. Some environmental campaigners, especially in America, believe that people have a psychological need for areas of "wilderness" in order to have such experiences.

Deep ecology shares this quest for self-actualisation, in that it rejects the image of our selves as isolated egos with boundaries separating us from the rest of the world. In philosophical terms there is no firm ontological divide in the field of existence. "To the extent that we perceive boundaries, we fall short of a deep ecological consciousness." (Warwick Fox)

Eastern roots

Much New Age thinking is rooted in Eastern philosophy. Capra writes of the "age-old notion of a fundamental universal rhythm resulting in fluctuating cultural patterns." Capra's own work draws extensively on Chinese Taoism.

According to Taoism, the universe is engaged in ceaseless motion and activity, a continual cosmic process known as "Tao", which means "the Way". Underlying the "rhythm of the universe" are the two archetypal poles, yin and yang, which set the limits for the cycles of change. Nothing is only yin or only yang – they are not categories dividing reality. All reality oscillates gradually between these poles, and is kept in a dynamic balance between them. Yin and yang are applied to human attitudes, seasons, and even food. Capra makes the following associations:

Yin	Yang
Earth	Heaven
Moon	Sun
Night	Day
Winter	Summer
Moisture	Dryness
Coolness	Warmth
Interior	Surface
Feminine	Masculine
Responsive	Aggressive
Cooperative	Competitive
Intuitive	Rational
Synthesising	Analytic

Friend or foe?

When Christians first became aware of the New Age movement there was considerable alarm in conservative evangelical circles. Some saw it as a global Satanic conspiracy and depicted the Green movement as part of this conspiracy, the New Age movement's "political wing".

Much of this criticism reflected the most conservative element of the church. Such critics have found it equally hard to accept other challenges to traditional thinking when breakthroughs have occurred in physics, biology and brain research.

Others have stressed the need to keep a sense of proportion. Later Christian critiques of the New Age movement have been more thoughtful and balanced. After all, Christians and New Age followers share certain beliefs, and reject the destructive, materialistic and utilitarian aspects of modern culture. Many Christians have previously held the mind in such high esteem that they have been negative towards the body, but now see a need to think holistically rather than dualistically. They thus share the New Age aim of integrating mind, body and spirit.

On the other hand, Christians are rightly wary because New Age thinking tends to be monist. Once a monist philosophy is adopted there can be no divine Being who is in any sense separate or transcendent. The impersonal universal power of pantheistic monism contrasts sharply with Christian belief in a supreme personal Being.

Moreover, ethical confusion often arises from pantheistic monism. The lack of differentiation between categories of existence and the absence of an external authority, make it difficult to explain wrongdoing and evil.

"Among the great spiritual traditions Taoism offers one of the most profound and most beautiful expressions of ecological wisdom, emphasizing both the fundamental oneness and the dynamic nature of all natural and social phenomena."
Fritjof Capra, *The Turning Point*

"Meeting with God involves personal encounter, not just a communing with the cosmos."
John Polkinghorne, *Science and Providence*

Christianity and the New Age movement both attempt to articulate a critical attitude towards our use of the Earth within a religious framework. Does our common interest mean that Christians should enter into friendly dialogue with New Age followers, or should we approach them more critically and proclaim our differences? What are the advantages and disadvantages of each?

SELF-REGULATING PLANET

A further religious foundation for people interested in ecology is paganism. Paganism is the belief in the divinity of Nature and all living things. Thus nature, containing its own divinity, regulates and directs itself.

Paganism

The term "pagan" is frequently misunderstood. It has come to mean "non-Christian", but more correctly describes followers of a traditional native religion who worship nature (the Latin root *paganus* means "country dweller").

Pagans perceive spirits in streams, rocks and groves. They believe that deities preside over love, inspiration, war and other activities. In order to heal a rift between humankind and the planet, pagans seek balance and harmony using the natural forces of the mind and the earth for healing and "rebalancing".

Paganism has the traditional characteristics of any religion – personal devotion, meetings, meditation, and seasonal festivities. Pagans have the equivalent of a priest – a "shaman" who acts as mediator between ordinary people and deities. They also perform rituals to alleviate starvation, military tension and environmental degradation.

Paganism is sometimes associated with witchcraft – the use of "supernatural" forces, either for good or for evil. In the Middle Ages, witches were sometimes known as "wise women", because their knowledge of nature made them skilled herbalists. But there were also witches who attempted to bring misfortune upon others through occult means (i.e. black magic). This led to witches being accused of making pacts with the devil.

Early Christian responses

How have Christians reacted to paganism?

In Britain, the first Christians absorbed many pagan rituals. Pagan festivals were incorporated into the Church's year. The name Easter, for example, is derived from the Anglo-Saxon spring goddess, Eostre. "The ancient worship of wells, trees and stones was not so much abolished as modified, by turning pagan sites into Christian ones and associating them with a saint rather than a heathen divinity." (Keith Thomas, *Religion and the Decline of Magic*)

Early Christianity in Britain appears to have been grounded in an appreciation of nature. This is especially evident in the Celtic Christian tradition.

Later the church became hostile towards pagan practices and in the 10th century they were outlawed. By the Middle Ages pagan deities were regarded by the church as demons, and pagans were considered devil worshippers.

WITCH-HUNT

During the 16th and 17th centuries there was a wave of witch-hunts across Europe, resulting in the execution of many thousands of people, mostly women. According to the most reliable authorities, around a thousand executions of alleged witches took place in Britain in this period.

Modern Pagans

Modern paganism takes two forms, the "wicca" religion, which has recently undergone a revival, and a more scientifically inspired belief in divinity within nature, based on the "Gaia hypothesis". The re-emergence of paganism today is sometimes interpreted as a spiritual response to the loss of a divine natural world. Some describe this new wave as "neo-paganism".

The revival of interest in paganism has been linked with the growth of eco-feminism, although not all eco-feminists are pagans. Parallels have been drawn between the oppression of women and destruction of "mother" nature. Much material written by protesters at the Greenham Common Peace Camp in the 1980s was explicitly pagan.

Some eco-feminists argue that women are more sensitive to nature with its seasonal cycles, because of their own bodily cycles. They are attracted to paganism because they see "feminine" attributes being suppressed in the Christian church. Paganism offers them an authority and status otherwise denied to them in the church.

The distinction between "white" magic and "black" magic is important. Contemporary pagans normally identify with the "wicca" religion, the practice of white magic ("wic" is derived from the Old English for "wisdom"). They dissociate themselves from black magic, deny belief in a devil, and vehemently reject any connection with Satanism.

Christian responses

Christians are warned in the Bible not to acknowledge or worship any deities in nature, nor to call upon any spiritual powers other than God. The Old Testament describes a conflict between the God of the Israelites and the pagan deities of the Canaanites, Baal and Asherah. God continually warned the Israelites against pagan idolatry (Ex 20:4 and 22:18, Deut 4:15-19, 7:5, 12:2-4, 18:10-11, Jer 10:1-11, 27:10).

There is, however, some common ground between Christians and pagans. Pagans see no division between matter and spirit, and reject the dualistic thinking which has wrongly influenced Christianity. They have a positive view of the Earth, regarding it as sacred and holy.

The need of some women to identify with a deity not defined in exclusively masculine language has long been recognised by pagans, who speak of the Earth as their "mother". Some Christians are now reappraising the traditional use of masculine imagery for God. Describing God in male terms may distance "Him" from them, especially if they have grown up with a negative image of their fathers. Thus the expression "the Motherhood of God" is being used to complement the traditional image of God as Father, though this remains very controversial.

Some Christians believe that the distinction between black and white magic is invalid because neither draws its power from God. Others argue that the use by white witches of nature's inherent healing qualities merely utilises God-given power for good. But white witches do not acknowledge the true source of nature's goodness; they invoke nature deities instead.

The cross on a hot cross bun once symbolised the four seasons. What justification is there for accepting into popular Christian practice folk customs which originated in paganism?

In addition to traditional Christian agricultural festivals, special liturgies have been developed in recent years to encourage Christians to celebrate seasonal change and thus the cycles of nature. Is this something to welcome, or to be wary of?

GOD AS GAIA

A rather different expression of paganism is a religious form of James Lovelock's "Gaia hypothesis". The hypothesis is that the right conditions exist for life on this planet because the Earth contains within it some kind of complex self-regulating mechanism. Although Gaia is the name of a Greek earth goddess, James Lovelock regarded the hypothesis as scientific and did not intend any religious interpretation.

There is, however, a long established religious belief that the Earth is a self-regulating living organism. Some people (notably Edward Goldsmith of *The Ecologist*) have elevated the Gaia hypothesis to a religious belief. The outcome could be described as "scientific paganism".

Goldsmith's *The Way: An Ecological World View* advances numerous hypotheses which are essentially pagan. The Earth, Gaia, is symbolised as a deity, self-regulating and the source of all of our benefits. The "central intuition" of Goldsmith's world view is that "Gaia is One" – awareness of the unity of all living things in the universe.

There have been attempts in past centuries to fuse Christianity with the idea that the Earth is a self-regulating living organism. But philosophers who did this, such as Giordano Bruno and Vladimir Solovyev, were frowned upon by the church. Bruno was burned at the stake in 1600, and the work of Solovyev in the 19th century was considered outside conventional Orthodox theology.

THE TRUTH OF SCIENCE

In industrialised countries it is often assumed that solutions to global environmental problems lie in efficient management and in applying the latest scientific research.

Greens incline towards ecocentrism (see pages 56-57), but most environmental policy-makers in industry and government tend to be technocentrists – they put their faith in science.

Such a faith was evident in a newspaper article on the Green movement by a former research ecologist at Oxford University. Dr John Horsfall, having poured scorn on dialogue between ecology and religion, concluded: "As a scientist I believe that the way out of the mess is through more and better science" (*The Guardian*, 20th April 1990).

"All science is certain, evident knowledge... We reject all knowledge which is merely probable."
Descartes

Such faith in science embodies the kind of optimism which emerged during the Enlightenment. Implicit in it is the possibility of scientific certainty, based on the predictability of particular courses of action.

The outcome of scientific study and reasoning is often considered to have greater validity than other approaches to knowledge. True knowledge is that which can be verified through observation. On the other hand, beliefs arrived at through emotion, intuition or spirituality, which cannot be "proved" through scientific methods such as empirical tests, are considered less valid – and sometimes completely dismissed.

Many scientists regard the mind as the main source of truth. Horsfall argued that "ecology has been hijacked by an astonishing range of irrationalists." He considered that the ideas of the Green movement were based on "mysticism, magic and fluffy philosophies", and he urged all who believed in the soundness of human reason not to ally themselves with it.

Is science objective?

Scientific research is important in identifying the exact cause of environmental problems. But would the environment be safe if put into the hands of the scientific community alone?

The objectivity of science is increasingly questioned. Since the start of the 20th century, scientists have become aware through quantum physics that their results are affected by the nature of the experiment. Thus subatomic units of matter appear as particles or waves according to how scientists look at them.

Social scientists have highlighted the implications of accepting that science is not "neutral". Scientists tend to see themselves as exploring "truth" with objectivity and detachment. Yet "most modern science is paid for by governments and businesses and is directed towards specific economic and political interests" (David Pepper, *The Roots of Modern Environmentalism*).

Relating science to religion

The relationship of science to religion has often been problematic. There has been much debate on whether science and religion are compatible. Often scientists have been resistant to interdisciplinary study of any kind.

From the 17th century onwards, scientific beliefs became a source of tension. The scientific method claimed to offer an unprecedented degree of certainty. It provided the basis for the claim that conclusions relating to the material world could be regarded as incontestable, whereas religious beliefs were less easy to "prove" and thus less certain. Rationality, the use of the mind in a logical, systematic process, was held in high regard, whereas intuition or emotion was considered of secondary importance.

In the 19th century people began to see an incompatibility between beliefs taught by the church and new ideas emerging from science, such as Darwin's theory of evolution. A gulf emerged between scientific materialists and Biblical literalists.

In the middle of the 20th century ecology became subject to debate between utilitarian scientists and others who adopted a more philosophical approach.

But more recently a new trend has emerged (see page 63). As doubts have arisen about scientific objectivity and certainty, some scientists (especially physicists) have begun exploring whether there is, after all, a place for God in their view of the universe.

Theologians, meanwhile, have reconsidered the relationship between traditional beliefs about creation and the findings of modern science, and have developed new approaches such as process theology (see page 31).

"Twentieth-century physics has shown us very forcefully that there is no absolute truth in science, that all our concepts and theories are limited and approximate."
Fritjof Capra, *The Turning Point*

EQUALLY VALUED

"Deep ecologists" (see page 58) take the belief that all life is interconnected (or "one") to mean that all life is of equal value. They would argue that it is not enough to acknowledge that human beings are part of nature. Human beings and other species need to be considered equal at every level. The insight that all life has value becomes the *idol of biocentric equality*.

Different species or organisms are normally valued according to their complexity and, hence, capacity for richness of experience. The principle of biocentric equality does not allow for any such hierarchy of value, whether based on skill, intellect or sentience.

The logic of biocentric equality is that human beings should avoid any use of other species. If all life is equal, people should be not merely vegetarians but vegans. Indeed, if all living organisms possess equal value, vegetables demand as much respect as animals. Yet when Buddhist Alan Watts was asked to comment on his dietary choice, he replied that he was a vegetarian because "cows scream louder than carrots."

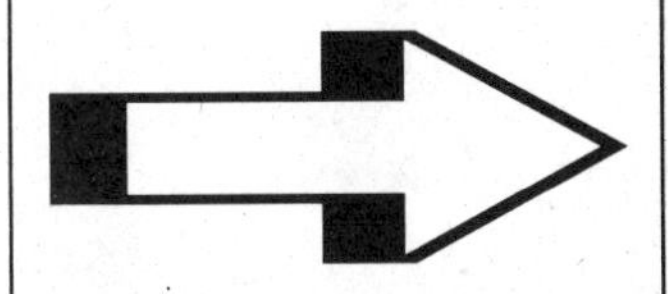

GOING FURTHER

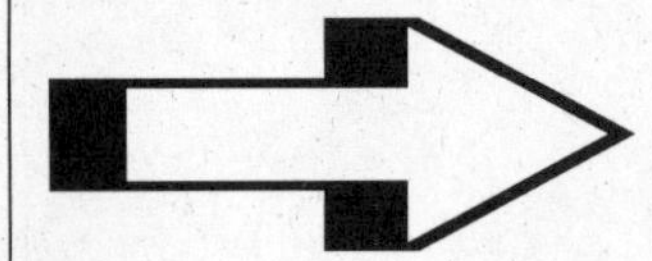

Christianity teaches that human beings are different from other species. We have been made in the image of God, a "little lower than the heavenly beings" (Gen 1:26, Ps 8:5). We are not just one strand in the web of life, but have distinct capabilities and responsibilities which are not shared by other species. It is upon our uniqueness that our special responsibility for the world rests.

Belief that all life is of equal value is not just unworkable but ultimately dangerous. There is a possibility that other species will not be treated as human beings, but human beings will be treated as non-sentient or unintelligent animals.

Additional reading

Christian critiques of environmental thought are hard to find. Stephen Clark's *How to Think About the Earth* is an authoritative study. Many of the beliefs described in this Unit are amplified in Tim Cooper's, *Green Christianity* (especially chapter 4), in Loren Wilkinson's chapter "New Age, New Consciousness, New Creation" in Wesley Granberg Michaelson's *Tending the Garden,* and in Ernest Lucas *Science and the New Age Challenge*. On the transformation of ideas into idols see Bob Goudzwaard, *Idols of our Times*. See also "Evangelicals and the Environment", a collection of essays in *Evangelical Review of Theology* Vol 17 No 2 April 1993.

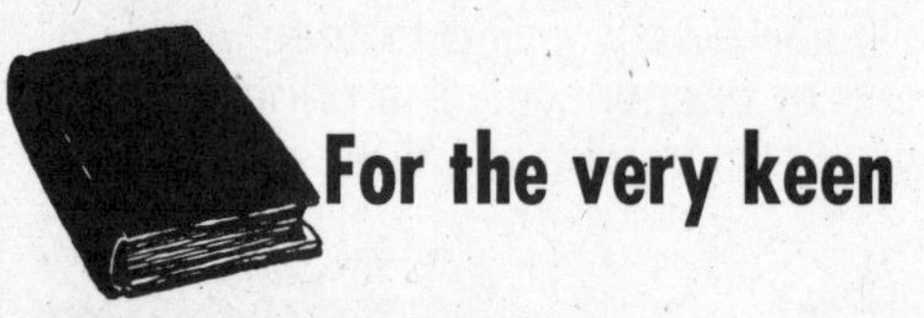

For the very keen

Martin Palmer, *Genesis or Nemesis*
An exploration of attitudes to the environment in the world's major religions. Discuss whether a cross-fertilisation of ideas among people of different faiths is essential if we are to find the insights and flexibility necessary to overcome the global environmental crisis.

Kevin Logan, *Paganism and the Occult*, Chapters 1-5, 9 & 13
An evangelical response to contemporary interest in paganism and the occult. Is there a "fuzzy edge" between the "soft" occult and hidden truths in Christianity? Does a fear of the kind of harmful spirituality described by Kevin Logan lead Christians to avoid a potentially beneficial exploration of God-given powers within nature and in mystical Christianity?

Russell Chandler, *Understanding the New Age*, Chapters 1-6, 9, 15, 21- 24 & 29-31
A well-informed and balanced study of the New Age movement. Identify and describe three principal factors which have influenced the growth of the New Age movement. How in practical terms should Christians address the challenges which it poses?

Peter Russell, *The Awakening Earth, Chapters* 3, 5, 6, 9-11 & 13
Peter Russell draws upon an ancient idea of the Earth as a self- regulating living organism, and raises the possibility of a major evolutionary step being stimulated by a change in human consciousness. Has the widely held Christian belief that the world will continue on an escalating downward spiral become a self-fulfilling prophecy? Or is Russell's thesis conceivably true?

Fritjof Capra, *The Turning Point, Chapters* 1, 2, 4, 5 & 10-12
One of the most influential critiques of modern Western culture. Does Capra's analysis provide convincing evidence that to create a healthy society we will find richer resources in Eastern thought than in the Christianity and science of the West?

SUSTAINING THE EARTH

UNIT 8

CHANGE HOW YOU LIVE!

CONTENTS

PURPOSE

The purpose of this Unit is to consider some practical environmental concerns which affect our lives today, and question how we might change our lifestyle so as to live with integrity in relation to them.

PRINCIPLES INTO PRACTICE

Some of the material used in this Unit is taken from Christian Ecology Link's resource pack *Steps Towards Sustainability* (£4 inc. p&p. For address see page 100). Also relevant is Chapter 8 in Tim Cooper, *Green Christianity*. There is a wide range of books on how to live in a more environmentally sensitive manner. The best of these include John Button, *How to be Green*, John Elkington and Julia Hailes, *The Green Consumer Guide*, and Karen Christianson, *The Green Home*.

How far is it possible for Christians to derive practical responses to environmental problems from their shared Christian beliefs?

Some years ago an Anglican report, *Man and Nature*, had the remit "to investigate the relevance of Christian doctrine to the problems of man in his environment." It noted that people expected churches to lay down general principles derived from theological insights, which they could then apply to particular situations.

The report's conclusion was challenging: "Either such principles have to be so general as to be quite ambiguous in application and therefore vacuous, or else they become so specific that they cannot be claimed to be the only possible Christian approach in every possible practical situation."

The church has often been wary of translating theological claims into practical action. And yet Christian belief should have a real and practical impact on our lives. Thinking through our theology enables us to define our faith which, unless it has an impact on our behaviour, is "dead" (Jam 2:17).

But how can we move from theological assertion to ethical imperative? From theology to discipleship? From theory to practice?

"We must do what we conceive to be the right thing and not bother our heads or burden our souls with whether we're going to be successful. Because if we don't do the right thing, we'll be doing the wrong thing, and we'll just be part of the disease and not a part of the cure."

E.F. Schumacher

From theology to discipleship

The process of exploring our understanding of God involves the use of concepts and models (often the tools of philosophy) to provide a framework within which to make moral and political judgements. The overall process may be depicted in a flow chart:

- Theology arises from our experience of God.
- But once we express that faith in words, we are immediately in dialogue with other things we "know", other "wisdom".
- This dialogue gives rise to Christian values and ethics in relation to our world.
- These in turn direct our moral attitudes and behaviour.

Key theological claims relating to ecology

- ❑ God is the creator of all things and is continually active in creation, sustaining life.
- ❑ All of nature's substances are good, all of life is significant, and the non-human creation has intrinsic value.
- ❑ God is revealed through nature and we may sense His presence through His creation.
- ❑ God's kingship qualifies, or limits, human dominion.
- ❑ Christianity must be understood within a 'holistic' framework.
- ❑ God calls us to exercise restraint in accumulating and consuming resources.
- ❑ We do not own the Earth but are responsible for taking care of it.
- ❑ We are redeemed with, not from, the created order.

Here are some key theological claims and some key ecological principles. Look at each claim in turn, and weigh up how far you agree with or identify with each. Mark each one ✖, ✔ or ?.

Then reflect on those you marked with a ✔. What guiding *values* for moral behaviour do you think these give rise to? Try to write them down at the foot of the page. These will help you evaluate the practical issues on the pages that follow.

Key principles derived from the scientific study of ecology

1. All organisms interact with their surroundings and cannot sustain life in isolation (interdependence).
2. The distribution of species may be inhibited by unfavourable environments (resistance).
3. All species tend to occupy a particular niche.
4. Natural systems recycle essential materials (e.g. carbon, nitrogen).
5. Natural systems evolve over time (succession and genetic change).
6. No population can increase without limit (carrying capacity).
7. Overexploited populations can collapse.
8. Ecosystems which are more complex tend to be more stable.

Values to guide moral behaviour in our care for the environment

(for example, Christians should avoid overpopulating the Earth)

The rest of this Unit covers six practical topics of current importance to the environment, and considers an appropriate Christian response to each. You will find suggestions for detailed reading on each of these topics at the end of the Unit. There are also some useful addresses which will allow you to follow up the topics in a more practical way.

Individuals will respond in different ways to the environmental challenge. Practical nature conservation projects, trying to live more simply, sharing resources, campaigning politically, growing food organically – all these are valid, practical expressions of concern. There is no perfect "model lifestyle". We need to allow for the diverse and varied operation of the Spirit of God.

AFFLUENCE

Upward pressure

The environmental impact of consumption is the key issue of the future. The Earth's life support systems are put under ever-increasing pressure as consumption rises throughout the world.

Yet consumption is the issue which most of us find hardest to face. There have always been people who seek to "live simply". But they remain a tiny fringe. The vast majority aspire to ever-higher incomes.

As industrial countries become richer their inhabitants do not necessarily become happier. "If everyone stands on tiptoe, no one sees better" (Fred Hirsch, *The Social Limits to Growth*).

Incomes and impacts

As a general rule, people with higher incomes tend to have a greater impact on the environment. But it's important not to confuse the financial world with the physical world.

The Bible suggests that we should seek lifestyles which enable poverty to be avoided but do not involve undue affluence:

- "Do not wear yourself out to get rich." (Prov 23:4)
- "Give me neither poverty nor riches." (Prov 30:8)
- "Better one handful with tranquillity than two handfuls with toil and chasing after the wind." (Ecc 4:6)
- "If we have food and clothing, we will be content with that." (1 Tim 6:8).

A THEOLOGY OF ENOUGH

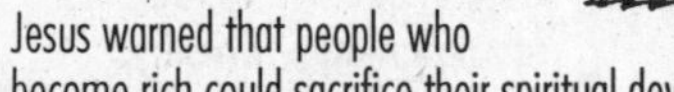

Jesus warned that people who become rich could sacrifice their spiritual development, as did the rich young man (Matt 19.16-29). He taught that "you cannot serve both God and Money" (Matt 6.24).

The Israelites were told that they should give generously to the poor (Deut 15:7-11). Jesus said that the rich should sell their possessions and give to the poor (Matt 19:21). The early Christians followed this teaching, giving to anyone in need (Acts 2:45).

For example, consuming less will reduce our physical impact on the world and save us money. But buying products that are "environmentally friendly" (e.g. organic food) or travelling by train rather than by car can be more expensive. Similarly, high quality consumer durables, such as furniture designed for durability or an energy-efficient fridge, will be relatively costly.

At a global level, it is important to treat data on average incomes with caution. A low cash income does not necessarily imply severe poverty. In some subsistence economies, people may have no cash incomes but have adequate food, water and housing. Access to fertile land for growing food is as important as cash.

Fair shares for all

The planet has a finite supply of raw materials and fossil fuels, and a limited capacity to absorb the waste and pollution which arises from consumption. At the Rio Earth Summit in 1992, the distribution of consumption between the rich countries of the "North" and the poor of the "South" became a key issue.

Scientists warn that emissions of carbon dioxide and other greenhouse gases must be reduced if the threat of global warming is not to increase. But as poorer countries industrialise, they inevitably consume more energy, including fossil fuels, and increase greenhouse gas emissions.

What does this imply at an international level? Countries in the "South" can hardly be expected to restrain their consumption when most of the damage has been caused by the "North". Global justice requires that rich countries cut back emissions of greenhouse gases by more than their "share", to allow for development in the "South".

Is prosperity a sign of God's favour?

Some Old Testament passages suggest that God brings material gain to those who obey Him (e.g. Deut 30:1-10). Christians have sometimes understood from such texts that if they are faithful to God then He will reward them in financial terms.

But this teaching must be understood in a historical context. The Israelites lived in an agrarian economy. Prosperity meant good harvests, not houses filled with consumer durables and a second car. There was not the potential for global environmental destruction as in the contemporary world.

It is dangerous to suggest that there is a necessary connection between people's relationship with God and their income. Individuals may simply be born into extreme poverty – this is not their fault. Nor is it when poverty arises as a result of political decisions taken at a national and international level, over which individuals have little control.

LIFESTYLE IMPLICATIONS

Consume less, give more

Question your level of consumption. Be generous to those in need. Has shopping become a habit? Can you differentiate your "needs" from your "wants"?

Be a green consumer

Be willing to pay more for products which are made with proper concern for the environment.

Ethical investment

Ensure that your savings, endowment policy, personal pension and any other investments are invested in a fund which is ethically screened.

Barter

Join one of the growing number of LETS (Local Exchange Trading Systems) schemes, which enable people to exchange skills (and products) outside the money economy.

"What were luxuries for our fathers have become necessities for us."

Reflection

- ☛ What is your annual income? Break your expenditure into components and identify, as far as possible, which of them are likely to have the most negative environmental impact. Draw up a plan to cut back on these over the next year. Repeat the exercise next year and monitor your progress.
- ☛ How does your income compare with the average income of other people in this country, and worldwide? Is your level of income "just"? What proportion of it do you spend on yourself, and how much do you give to others?

GLOBAL FACTS

- The world has over 3 million millionaires.
- A third of the world's population lack access to clean water.

NATIONAL FACTS

Average Weekly Household Consumption and CO_2 emissions from Energy Use:

Fuel	144kg CO_2
Car (if any)	71kg CO_2
Water	2,350 litres
Wood	35cm^3
Steel	11kg
Aluminium	1kg
Meat	5lbs
Vegetables	10lbs

(Source: Ethical Consumer magazine)

ENERGY

GLOBAL FACTS

Energy consumption has increased fourfold worldwide over the past four decades, from 3.26TW in 1950 to 13.73TW in 1990.

Carbon dioxide accounts for around 55% of the known impact of greenhouse gases, CFCs and halons 24%, methane 15%, nitrous oxide 6%.

There are many ways in which our use of energy has a negative impact on the planet – and the Earth's reserves of fossil fuels are finite.

Global warming

Our excessive use of energy is causing global warming. The danger is that sea levels will rise, causing the flooding of low-lying regions. Also, consequent changes in regional weather patterns could have a dramatic, negative impact on food production.

A reduction of emissions of greenhouse gases of at least 60% is required to offset this threat, according to the world's leading authority, the *Intergovernmental Panel on Climate Change*.

Pollution and health

The effect on people's health of air pollution from energy-related sources has become an increasing concern.

Vehicle fumes are believed to be responsible for the growing incidence of asthma among children. There are fears that emissions of dioxins from "waste-to-energy" incinerators will cause cancer. Radiation from nuclear reactors has been blamed for leukaemia.

Finite supplies

The Earth has a limited supply of fossil fuels such as oil, gas and coal. According to a *Scientific American* report, there are enough global reserves of oil to last 35 years at current rates of consumption. Total oil resources, including those which currently cannot be extracted profitably, would last 83 years. These timescales will shorten if consumption continues to increase.

Renewable sources of energy such as wind power, wave power and geothermal power are widely regarded as more environmentally acceptable. However virtually all publicly funded research on alternatives to fossil fuels has been on nuclear power.

The relationship between God and the natural world, expressed in terms of energy, can contribute a theological foundation to the debate on energy use.

Theologian Ruth Page describes this as follows: "The presence and activity (*energeia*) of God represent 'uncreated energy', an omnipresent, undegradable energy, to which the second law of thermodynamics does not apply. 'Created energies', on the other hand, at micro and macro levels, keep creation dynamic and active." These created energies have come into being in response to the uncreated energy.

The term "synergy" describes two energies working together. Creation flourishes when the created energies co-operate with the Creator, in "divine synergy".

This theological foundation has moral implications. As the aim of such synergy is fullness of life (John 10:10), one test of an energy policy is whether it enhances life or is wasteful and destructive.

"No degree of prosperity could justify the accumulation of large amounts of highly toxic substances which nobody knows how to make 'safe' and which remain an incalculable danger to the whole of creation."

E.F. Schumacher, *Small is Beautiful*

NATIONAL FACT

The average household spends £50 each week on fuel. According to the Government around £10 of this could be saved cost-effectively.

Nuclear power – an acceptable option?

Perhaps the most controversial of energy subjects is nuclear power.

✔ **Advocates** argue that the possibility of using energy by splitting the atom has been structured into creation by the Creator. They point out that nuclear energy drives the sun and other stars, and suggest that in utilising such power we are merely using our God-given creativity.

✖ **Critics** question this. They argue that it is irresponsible to tamper with the building blocks of matter with such potential for causing widespread environmental destruction. They express a concern about links between nuclear power and nuclear weapons, and highlight problems raised by radioactive waste and the need to decommission nuclear reactors.

The case for nuclear power largely rests upon whether it is *safe, cheap and necessary*.

❶ **Safe**: Advocates argue that in the industrialised West nuclear power has an excellent safety record. They reject claims that it involves more risk than the use of chemicals and other toxic substances.

Objectors point out that there have been several occasions when a "melt down" has only been narrowly avoided. Even if the risk of an accident were infinitesimal the case for nuclear power is weak, because it is not the magnitude of the risk that is significant but the scale of the potential damage. The doctrine of the fall means that human beings are fallible and no nuclear reactor can be wholly safe.

❷ **Cheap**: Supporters of nuclear power once argued that it would create electricity "too cheap to meter".

By the 1980s, however, it became clear that electricity from nuclear reactors is more costly than that from gas fired power stations. It is in any case widely agreed that investment in energy conservation would be more cost-effective.

❸ **Necessary**: The nuclear power industry points out that its electricity does not contribute significantly to climate change. They claim that it is "unrealistic" to stop scientific development.

Critics respond that our future energy requirements could be met without nuclear power. There are alternatives to burning fossil fuels, apart from nuclear energy – such as energy conservation and the use of renewable energy.

Reflection

☛ Do you find the case for retaining Britain's nuclear power programme convincing?

LIFESTYLE IMPLICATIONS

Buy energy efficient products

Energy efficient light bulbs use a small fraction of the energy of traditional light bulbs and last much longer. Refrigerators consume a lot of energy, so choose an energy efficient model.

Insulate

Reduce your heating costs by insulating your loft and any cavity walls, lagging the hot water tank, using thermostatic and timer controls, and fitting curtains with thermal linings. Set the temperature as low as is comfortable and wear more clothes if needed.

Minimise electricity consumption

Avoid electrical products as far as possible. Use gas for cooking and heating, as two-thirds of energy is wasted in generating electricity. Turn off unnecessary lights.

ANIMAL WELFARE

Low status

Throughout history animals have been ill-treated. They have often been regarded as unthinking, unfeeling machines rather than as sentient, living beings. Even today most people value animals according to their usefulness. Environmentalists believe that all animals possess intrinsic value (which does not, of course, mean they are of equal worth). Our perception of the differences between ourselves and other animals will affect how we treat them. Do we have an empathy for other animals?

Rights?

The issue of animal rights has rapidly risen up the political agenda. Opposition to factory farming, hunting, animal experiments and the export of live animals has grown in strength. Whereas in the past people spoke of their concern for the *welfare* of animals, they are now equally likely to use the language of *rights*. But do animals have rights?

The question of rights is about a reciprocal relationship in which one party has a "just claim" to be treated well and the other has a responsibility to act accordingly. Rights have to be agreed or granted.

One objection to the language of rights is that they are not agreed by the animals but by human beings. Theologian Andrew Linzey argues that animals have a right to reasonable treatment because they have been created and are sustained by God. This right belongs to God rather than the animals.

Reasons to act

Some people choose to become vegetarians or reduce their meat intake because of the abuse of farm animals, a desire to improve their health by reducing their fat intake, or concern at the amount of land needed to produce meat. A few go further and become vegans, rejecting any product derived from animals.

Hunting and animal experimentation are two other issues which attract concern. Objections to hunting are based on the innocence of the victim and claims of cruelty. Critics of experiments on animals argue that they are often duplicated unnecessarily, and that results are unreliable due to differences between human beings and other animals.

A further issue is genetic engineering. Selective breeding has taken place throughout history, but genetic engineering speeds up the process. There has been pressure for animals which have had their genes manipulated to be patented, effectively allowing a species to be "owned". Some animals bred with manipulated genes have suffered serious physical defects.

Should Christians be vegetarians?

God's original intention may have been for all living creatures to have a vegetarian diet (see Gen 1:29, cf. Gen 9:3). However, the Israelites ate meat (Deut 12:15). Jesus, in all probability, did too; he certainly ate fish (Matt 14:17, Luke 24:42-3) and the gospels would surely have mentioned it if he did not eat meat.

Paul taught that Christians could eat meat (Rom 14:14, 1 Cor 10:25, 1 Tim 4:3-4) and even suggested that in some circumstances vegetarianism was a sign of weakness (Rom 14:2). However he also wrote that "everything is permissible - but not everything is beneficial" (1 Cor 10:23) and identified circumstances in which it would be better not to eat meat (Rom 14:13-21).

The morality of eating meat has to be considered in the context of contemporary farming practices. Anyone eating meat from animals reared on factory farms helps to sustain a production system which abuses creatures valued by God.

Animal welfare is considered a fringe issue by most Christians. Yet we have a responsibility to care for animals, as they have intrinsic value by virtue of being created by God.

Souls
Many Christians have argued that animals lack souls and are therefore not worthy of moral concern, although the Bible does not dismiss the possibility that animals are spirit-filled (Ecc 3:21).

C.S. Lewis responded that if they lack souls, in the sense of having no moral responsibilities and immortality, the infliction of pain on them is harder to justify, as it would mean that they cannot deserve pain, nor profit morally from the discipline of pain, nor be recompensed by happiness in another life.

Relationships
Our commitment to right relationships (or "shalom") should apply to animals as well as to other people. There is a "spiritual continuity" between human beings and other living creatures. We have dominion over them, but like them we are dependent upon the Spirit of God for life (Gen 1:28, Ps 104:27-30).

Practice
Human beings have been given a mandate to rule over other creatures (Gen 1:26-28). We will, however, be held accountable for our treatment of them, as "the Earth is the Lord's, and everything in it" (Ps 24:1). Several Old Testament laws appear designed to prevent cruelty to animals. For example, newly born animals were not to be taken from their mothers (Lev 22:26-27). Bird life was protected (Deut 22:6-7). Animals were to be allowed rest (Ex 20:10).

Proper treatment is linked to righteousness: "A righteous man cares for the needs of his animal" (Prov 12:10). Jesus reminded his followers that God was concerned for all species, even sparrows (Luke 12:6,24).

GLOBAL FACT

Around 100 billion animals are killed worldwide each year through farming and animal experimentation. The human population is below 6 billion.

NATIONAL FACTS

A clergyman, Arthur Broome, convened the meeting which set up the RSPCA. It was attended by the evangelical social reformer William Wilberforce.

The average size of flocks of chickens being reared for meat is 22,000. Around 96% of egg-laying hens are kept in cages measuring 20" by 18", with four or more birds in each cage.

LIFESTYLE IMPLICATIONS

"The lamb misused breeds public strife And yet forgives the butcher's knife."
William Blake

Eat less meat
Cut back on meat and eat other sources of protein (e.g. pulses, dairy produce). Avoid chicken and pork where the animals have been factory farmed.

Choose cruelty-free products
Only buy eggs labelled "free range". If possible obtain them from a locally known producer rather than a supermarket. Buy cosmetics which have not been tested on animals.

Praise God for animals
Cathedrals and other churches sometimes hold services for intercession and the blessing of animals, often organised by Christian animal welfare organisations.

Help local wildlife
Encourage hedgehogs, birds and other wildlife in your garden. Support campaigns to protect local sites threatened with unnecessary building development.

Reflection

- Some people act as if we have the right to treat animals in whatever way we choose. Others believe that as far as possible we should avoid any use of them. Where do you draw the line, and why?
- Why do you think that relatively few Christians are in the forefront of the animal welfare movement?

CAR USE

Upward spiral

Mrs Thatcher once spoke of the "great car economy". In recent decades there has been a huge growth in car travel, and in 1989 the Government began to plan for a doubling of road traffic by the year 2025. More recently it has been recognised that such growth is not sustainable.

The trend towards car use is self-perpetuating. People drive cars because the roads are dangerous for cyclists and pedestrians. Their decision to drive increases traffic and makes more cyclists resort to cars and more parents to driving their children around. Similarly, when fewer people use public transport, revenue received by bus and rail operators falls, forcing prices up and causing further reductions in demand.

GLOBAL FACT

There are over 400 million cars on the road. Each car engine emits around 1,000 chemical compounds, with results varying from the well-documented to the completely unknown.

Little has been written about the car from a Christian perspective. A decade ago Christian sociologist Tony Walter questioned the use of cars. He pointed out that there is a moral dimension to the use of cars, as with any technology. It is "right at the centre of what politics is all about: power and powerlessness."

More recently in the magazine *Third Way* Catherine von Ruhland suggested that Christians should consider the environmental and social impacts of cars, and stop thinking of car ownership as a blessing.

In the mid-1990s the Evangelical Alliance's *Creation Care Group* promoted an annual day of rest for cars, known as "Car Free Sunday". The aim was to encourage Christians to care for the environment by not driving to church. It was also hoped that Christians would reflect on their use of cars at other times.

Environmental impact

The use of cars is increasingly criticised because of the environmental damage caused.

Emissions from car exhausts harm people susceptible to heart or lung disease (including asthma and bronchitis) and cause eye and nose irritation. They also contribute to acid rain. Carbon dioxide emitted by burning petrol or diesel is a major greenhouse gas.

Car use also depletes finite energy and raw material supplies. Fuel used in cars accounts for a high and rising proportion of oil consumption, depleting supplies of a vital but non-renewable resource.

Visual blight is another problem. New roads require the mining of aggregates, sometimes in areas of considerable beauty. Multi-storey car parks hide more attractive buildings. Rows of parked cars make town centres unsightly.

Community effects

The demise of strong and healthy communities is partly attributable to the car.

People without cars tend to be less affluent. Their misfortune increases when planners assume that people have cars, and make access to shops and other facilities inconvenient and costly for those without them.

Friendship between neighbours, which helps to bind a community, is less likely if people never walk past their neighbours' houses.

Once car ownership reaches a certain point, public transport is not viable, small shops close, and local employment becomes scarce as traders relocate to commercial districts situated outside town centres.

Convenience, freedom, privacy?

People own cars because of their potential to save time and effort. But in practice such savings may not be achieved. People spend more time travelling in countries where car ownership is high, because society becomes structured around the mobile car users.

Cars are supposed to bring freedom, but instead their use can lead to dependence. They do not provide a solution to people's actual need, which is to be "somewhere else". Mobility is simply a means to an end.

Cars are closely associated with status, many being a company perk. In a culture characterised by increased individualism, people want to show off affluence but to retain privacy. Cars fulfil this need; they are costly but enable privacy, shelter and separation from society.

NATIONAL FACTS

Although there are around 23 million cars on the road in Britain, almost a third of all households do not own one... yet!

Around 50% of women do not have a driving licence.

"What does our addiction to the car tell our children? That our convenience and comfort are more important than other people's? That keeping ourselves to ourselves is better than mixing with strangers? That getting there is all that matters, and the quicker the better?

Catherine von Ruhland

LIFESTYLE IMPLICATIONS

Minimise driving

Avoid using a car whenever possible, especially for short local journeys. Ride a bicycle or use public transport. Consider car sharing, perhaps with a neighbour or friend, and offer lifts whenever possible.

Live close

Consider the implications of moving to a new locality which may lock the family into car dependence. Avoid long-distance commuting.

Shop locally

Use local shops, especially for fruit and vegetables, which are more likely to be grown locally than those bought in supermarkets. Avoid out-of-town shopping centres.

Campaign for change

Put pressure on decision-makers in government for alternatives to the car: an expansion of public transport, more cycle lanes and bus lanes, and restrictions on lorries.

Drive with care

Do not exceed 50 mph, as this speed minimises your energy consumption. Turn off your engine if you are stationary for more than a few minutes. Avoid driving when pollution levels are high.

Reflection

Write three reasons which people use to justify owning a car. How would you argue against them?

List three measures which could be taken in your locality to reduce people's need of cars.

POPULATION

Growth

All generations are, by definition, interconnected. The lifestyle, activities and behaviour of the present generation will have a powerful impact on the wellbeing of future generations.

Even if significant progress is made in the availability of family planning, the world's population will continue to rise for many years. United Nations projections suggest that it will increase from 5 billion in 1987 to 8 billion between 2015 and 2045, and ultimately to over 10 billion before stability is achieved.

Population is increasing fastest in African and Middle Eastern countries, but is also rising in many high-consumption industrialised countries.

GLOBAL FACT

During Jesus' life-time the world's population is estimated to have been 250 million. It reached 1,000 million during the first half of the eighteenth century. It is now fast approaching 6,000 million.

Christians have sometimes taught that people have a God-given right, even a duty, to bear children. Some are motivated by the prospect of an increase in the proportion of children with Christian upbringings. The 1968 Roman Catholic Encyclical *Humanae Vitae* proclaimed: "Each and every marriage act must remain open to the transmission of life."

The Old Testament appears to encourage procreation. God told the first man and woman to "be fruitful and increase in number; fill the earth and subdue it" (Gen 1:28). The same message is restated more than a dozen times in the first five books of the Bible. Other texts reinforce the belief that children are a sign of God's blessing (e.g. Deut 7:13, Ps 107:38).

But are these texts directly applicable to contemporary society?

The cultural context must be taken into account: the population today is at least twenty times greater than when the Old Testament was written. Many more generations may need to live on the planet.

Significantly, the emphasis in the New Testament changes from physical to spiritual fruitfulness.

The environment connection

Rapid population growth undermines sustainable development because the Earth's "carrying capacity" is limited. For example, as numbers increase, pressure on land can result in soil degradation. In many cities in poor countries, numbers are rising rapidly yet the existing infrastructure is already inadequate, pollution is appalling, and there are far too few jobs.

Each additional person in industrialised countries has a disproportionate impact on the Earth's finite resources and capacity to absorb pollutants. Hence, concludes David Carter: "The comfortable belief that overpopulation is purely a Third World problem must be challenged."

If every person on the planet consumed as much as those in industrialised countries, an intolerable strain would be put on the global environment. Although this is a hypothesis which will not become a reality, it suggests that on ethical grounds we should be the first to act.

Choice

Many people, even in affluent countries, remain poorly informed about contraception, resulting in many millions of unplanned children being born each year.

In poor countries many people do not need to be convinced of the benefits of smaller families. But a very high proportion of women who do not want more children lack access to effective birth control methods and facilities.

Each child should be wanted by its parents, but many Christians will regard abortion as a means of population control indefensible.

How are poverty and population connected?

Some development campaigners do not regard population as a critical issue. They believe that families will choose to have fewer children once they have a secure income, child mortality is reduced, and the status and education of women is improved. They argue that most environmental damage is caused by a relatively small number of people and corporations.

Others, however, regard population growth as an urgent problem, a potential "time-bomb" which threatens economic progress in the poorest countries. If population growth exceeds income growth, income per head falls. Some experts fear that a reduction in family size in response to increased incomes will not be enough, and insist that additional measures to reduce population growth are required.

The reality is that poverty and population both need to be addressed. The policies required are not mutually exclusive.

Roman Catholic missionary Sean McDonagh advocates birth control, against the teaching of his church. But he warns that if it is not accompanied by land reform and development aid, it becomes "an oppressive tool in the hands of the rich" (Sean McDonagh, *To Care for the Earth*).

LIFESTYLE IMPLICATIONS

Plan your numbers
As newly married couples, plan in advance how many children you want in your family. Consider your motives carefully in deciding whether to add to your family.

Consider natural contraception
Natural methods of contraception are much better understood and explained than in the past. Couples are more likely to understand and appreciate the woman's natural bodily cycles. Such methods enable women to avoid regularly taking drugs in the form of the pill.

Campaign for global justice
Add your voice to pressure from development and aid organisations for more assistance to help poor countries achieve appropriate, environmentally sustainable development.

Reflection

- Why has population not been a major political issue in Britain? Would you favour measures to reduce our population and, if so, which ones?
- Consider the proposition that people who advocate living in harmony with nature should regard the use of contraceptives as unnatural and let nature take its course. Is there an ecological case for the Catholic Church's teaching?

NATIONAL FACT

The UK population continues to increase. Between 1990 and 2010 it is likely to grow by around a million.

"The power of population is so superior to the power of the earth to provide subsistence... that premature death must in some shape or other visit the human race."
Revd Thomas Malthus

WASTE

A waste mountain

The volume of waste generated in our "throw-away society" is large and increasing. Municipal waste per head in the industrialised West has increased by around a quarter over the past decade.

Households in Britain discard around 20 million tonnes of waste each year. This is only a small proportion of the total waste generated – over 400 million tonnes. A tiny fraction of household waste (around 5%) is recycled. A similar amount is incinerated. The remaining 90% is dumped in landfill sites.

Waste poses a multitude of problems. Some of it contains toxic materials. Some is radioactive. The transportation of waste, often by lorries, adds to an already excessive burden on roads. In many areas landfill sites are filling up. People are beginning to wonder what we will do in years ahead with all the waste generated.

Won't people be put out of work?

A traditional response to the argument that consumption must be reduced is that this will increase unemployment. If fewer products and services are demanded, less people will be needed to make them.

But this assumption is increasingly questioned. Sustained economic growth over the past decade has not eradicated unemployment. "Jobless growth" suggests that there is no direct correlation between output and employment. Businesses often expand by investing in labour-saving equipment, and increased consumption may create jobs overseas where many consumer durables are produced.

By contrast, a "conserver" economy – in which products are repaired rather than replaced, buildings are properly insulated, and trade is developed within the local community – is likely to provide additional employment opportunities.

Waste as wealth

Waste is discarded because it is seen as something which is worthless. But increasingly it is recognised that much of what is thrown away has a hidden value. The problem is that there has not been the necessary investment in the infrastructure and equipment required to extract value from discarded items by repairing or recycling them.

Prices do not always tell the "ecological truth". Virgin raw material prices do not take full account of the environmental impact of extraction and transportation.

At the same time, reducing waste (by, for example, insulating houses and repairing household products) is often a labour intensive process. It is consequently costly in high wage, industrialised countries.

Environmental economists favour "ecological tax reform", by which taxes would be switched from the use of labour to the use of energy and raw materials. The price of energy and raw material inputs would increase, deterring waste, while labour costs would fall, thus making repair work cheaper.

Beyond recycling

Recycling is one solution to excessive waste. But even recycling has an impact on the environment, as materials have to be collected and then manufactured into new products.

Environmentalists are pointing to the need to go beyond recycling. They argue that products should be made to last longer, that repairs should be encouraged, and that packaging and functionable components from discarded products should be reused. As the environmental costs of consumption are recognised, the throw-away society is being challenged.

In Nottingham a scheme was launched in 1993 to mobilise churches into environmental action by presenting them with an opportunity to participate in recycling.

The City Council saw a potential for church involvement in recycling centres because they are numerous, sited in the centre of communities, may have spare land which can accommodate facilities, and can offer volunteers to help with coordination and organisation.

The project has been developed by voluntary workers from a Diocesan Volunteer Scheme. Study packs and children's books on environmental issues written from a Christian perspective were distributed to local churches to raise interest. A video entitled *How Green is Your Church?* was produced and made available free of charge to local churches. Talks were offered.

By 1995 ten churches, from several denominations, were actively involved. Six had adopted recycling sites, three others had mini-recycling centres on their premises, and one was carrying out a kerbside collection scheme. Participating churches are paid an annual sum, some of which has to be spent on environmental projects such as fitting energy efficient light bulbs.

Over eighty churches are involved in the Nottingham Churches Environment Network. They regularly distribute several thousand newsheets on Christian responses to environmental issues, and hold quarterly meetings.

GLOBAL FACT

Many thousands of people in urban areas in poor countries make a living by sorting out rubbish by hand, sometimes in appalling conditions on waste dumps.

NATIONAL FACTS

- The Government has set a target for 25% of domestic waste to be recycled by the year 2000.
- A survey found that half the electrical goods discarded at civic amenity sites still functioned or could easily be repaired.

LIFESTYLE IMPLICATIONS

Reduce waste

Reduce unnecessary consumption and waste. Share vehicles, appliances and tools with family, friends and neighbours. Choose reusable packaging, including milk bottles rather than cartons, and durable carrier bags.

Increase recycling

Recycle every item that local authorities will accept, especially food and drink containers. Make compost using waste from the kitchen and garden.

Recycle with care

It is counterproductive to use additional energy in order to recycle. Avoid making special visits by car to recycling centres. Don't rinse food and drink containers with freshly heated water.

Make things last longer

Repair your possessions rather than discarding them. Buy second hand products. Choose quality rather than quantity.

"When materials and energy are 'used up' during the making and consuming of goods and services nothing disappears, rather, everything given enough time reappears somewhere in the environment."

Kerry Turner

Reflection

Empty the contents of your dustbin onto the ground. Separate them into different materials, including high quality paper, newspaper, plastic, metal, glass, organic matter. What proportion of the total is accounted for by each? Consider in turn *why* each item or material was not recycled or reused.

GOING FURTHER

Affluence

Rich Christians in an Age of Hunger by Ronald Sider is a classic study of Christian principle and practice. Alan Thein Durning's *How Much is Enough?* is a thought-provoking book which has influenced the "sustainable consumption" debate. Mike Starkey's *Born to Shop* is an amusing Christian view of our shopping culture. Also relevant are Chapters 3 and 6 in Tim Cooper's *Green Christianity* and Paul Brand's essay "A Handful of Mud" in Wesley Granberg-Michaelson (ed), *Tending the Garden*.

Energy

John Houghton, a Christian and former head of the Meteorological Office, has written *Global Warming*. The Church of Scotland's Society, Religion and Technology Project has published a report, *Scorching Heat and Drought*. *Christian Action Journal* produced a special issue on Energy in Winter 1993. There is a wide range of books on energy from a scientific or political perspective, such as M. Grubb's *Energy Policies and the Greenhouse Effect*.

Animal Welfare

Theologian Andrew Linzey has written prolifically on Christian attitudes to animals. His book, *Animal Theology*, and the earlier *Christianity and the Rights of Animals*, are well worth obtaining. See also Chapter 7 in Tim Cooper, *Green Christianity*.

Car use

Catherine von Ruhland's article "Driving Britain to the Brink", appeared in the July 1994 edition of *Third Way*. Environmental critiques of the car include Paul Nieuwenhuis' *The Green Car Guide*.

Population

Roy McCloughry has written a Grove Booklet *Population Growth and Christian Ethics*. Catholic priest Sean McDonagh tackles the population issue in *The Greening of the Church*. Dave Carter's article "Unnumbered Blessings" appeared in the October 1991 edition of *Third Way*. A leading secular text is Paul and Anne Ehrlich's *The Population Explosion*.

Waste

Jan McHarry's book *Reuse, Repair, Recycle* is a useful practical guide to reducing your impact on the environment. *Beyond Recycling,* a report for the New Economics Foundation by Tim Cooper, puts the case for making longer-lasting products a higher priority than recycling.

USEFUL ADDRESSES

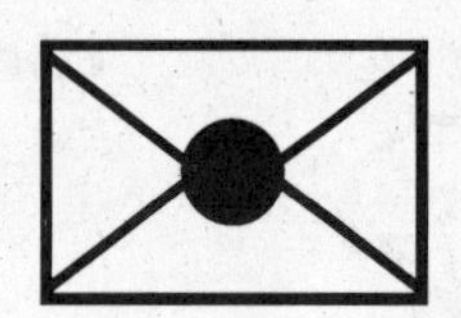

General

- *Christian Ecology Link*, 20 Carlton Road, Harrogate HG2 8DD.
- *UK Evangelical Environmental Network, St Peter's Church, Vere Street, London W1M 9HP.*
- *Third Way*, St Peter's, Sumner Road, Harrow HA2 4BX.

Affluence

- *Lifestyle*, 21 Fleetwood Court, West Byfleet, Surrey KT14 6BE (network for people trying to live simply).
- *Ethical Investment Research Service*, 504 Broadway Business Centre, 71 Broadway, London SW8 1SQ.
- *LETSLink UK*, 61 Woodcock Road, Warminster, Wilts BA12 9DH.
- *Ethical Consumer magazine*, 41 Old Birley Street, Manchester M15 5RF.
- *The New Economics Foundation*, Vine Court, 112-116 Whitechapel Road, London E1 1JE.

Animal welfare

- *Animal Christian Concern* can be contacted at 46 St Margaret's Road, Horsforth Road, Leeds LS18 5BG.
- *The Real Meat Company*, which supplies meat from animals reared humanely, is based at East Hill Farm, Heytesbury, Warminster, Wilts BA12 0HR.

Car use

- The *Evangelical Alliance Creation Care Group* is based at Whitefield House, 186 Kennington Park Road, London SE11 4BT.

Waste

- *Friends of the Earth's* local groups are often well informed about recycling and reuse initiatives. They can be contacted through libraries or FoE's head office at 26-28 Underwood Street, London N1 7JQ.

SUSTAINING THE EARTH

UNIT 9

ENVIRONMENT AND THE CHURCH

CONTENTS

PURPOSE

The purpose of this Unit is to suggest ways in which Christians actively concerned for the environment may act collectively through their churches.

A GREEN WITNESS IN THE WORLD?

What is the role of churches in relation to the environment? Do they have a responsibility to teach their members about environmental issues? Should they advocate, or even take, political action? How can they encourage changes in lifestyle, among their members and in society?

More power than you think

Churches witness to God by living as "communities of visibly redeemed creation" (Larry Rasmussen). Our faith should materially affect the world. It should have a transforming impact.

Christianity is the most powerful religion in the industrial West. The West is where consumption is excessive, which is the source of many environmental problems.

Christian churches thus have a special responsibility for the Earth. "The world economic situation today is particularly embarrassing for Christians. The 1.5bn followers of Jesus, 'who had no place to lay his head' now control two-thirds of the Earth's resources" (Sean McDonagh, *To Care for the Earth*).

Our affluence and influence is so great that, if the wealth and power of church members in industrial countries was distributed as suggested by Biblical teaching, the international economy and perhaps also the condition of the global environment would be radically transformed.

Signs of the kingdom

The vitality of Christianity is sometimes lost because of a misguided fatalism – a belief that our fallen state rules out any prospect of improvement in the world around us. Despair at the sheer scale of social and environmental problems results in inactivity.

Yet through its witness the Church should be revealing God's purpose for creation. The apostle Paul pictures the whole creation waiting for "those who are led by the Spirit of God" to be revealed so that creation can "be liberated from its bondage to decay" (Rom 8:12-25).

While we await the coming of the kingdom of God in its full glory, we should seek to create a "provisional" kingdom, signs of the rule of God which provide a foretaste of heaven (2 Cor 5:17).

A question of integrity

The church is often compromised by inconsistency between what it preaches and what is practised by its members. We need integrity. If Christians in their corporate life do not set a good example in their use of creation, the whole Christian witness is weak. Our proclamation about the coming of the God's kingdom will sound hollow and we will stand accused of hypocrisy.

Changing attitudes and behaviour is unlikely to be quick or easy, either within the Church or outside it. Even when the Church acts with integrity in respect of the environment, it cannot expect to change the world in an instant and produce an ecological utopia.

But Christian action is not just about achieving outcomes. "My calling is to be faithful to the Lord in this and all other aspects of my life, and to leave the outcome to him" (Rowland Moss, *The Earth in Our Hands*).

The worldwide Church

The Church joins people throughout the world into a single communion – a potent symbol of global interconnectedness. The apostle Paul used the metaphor of the Church as a "body" made up of parts linked together for mutual benefit (1 Cor 12:12-31).

Peace and justice have long been on the international agenda of the Church. The World Council of Churches' *Justice, Peace and the Integrity of Creation* initiative in the late 1980s did much to raise the profile of environmental concerns. More needs to be done.

Many Christians working overseas in evangelism or aid and development work operate in areas where environmental destruction is acute, such as rain forests and desert regions. Christians in industrialised countries need to know more about the needs of such areas. Perhaps there is a need for an international network of Christians with an interest in environmental problems.

Denominational structures

At a denominational level, different churches have responded to environmental questions with varying degrees of success.

The Church of England's General Synod has issued statements about the need to engage in environmental stewardship, but the Church's own record is regarded by many environmentalists as unimpressive. As one of Britain's largest landowners it allows hunting and intensive farming on its land despite public disquiet. Such practices have been discussed by General Synod but recent attempts to phase them out failed. Meanwhile little or no effort appears to have been made to encourage organic farming.

The Church Commissioners, who act on the Church of England's behalf in financial matters, claim to take ethical criteria into effect in their investments. Other Christians and ethical investment experts are unimpressed. A court case brought by the Bishop of Oxford revealed that the Commissioners do not take ethical criteria into account in their investment decisions if there is any likelihood of a reduced financial return.

Christian Ecology Link has established "denominational teams" to promote environmental interest in the major denominations.

St Egbert's Action Plan

1. We must be visible

We will monitor the local news – environmental problems periodically arise in every part of the country. We will be seen to take an interest in local issues and oppose environmental degradation.

2. We must get informed

Before speaking out on any environmental concern, we will make certain we are aware of the facts and familiar with both sides of the argument. We must be sure of the ethical foundations of our position.

3. We must speak with integrity

We will take steps to reduce the environmental impact of our church's activities, and avoid being hypocritical. We will carry out an ecological audit.

4. We must act at the top

We will find out about any environmental initiative being taken by our denominational headquarters. We will respond to information about any of the church's future activities which may affect the environment.

TAUGHT TO THINK AGAIN

One of the primary tasks of the Church is to teach, encourage, inspire and empower Christians to live out their faith in the world. This is especially important in relation to the environment if, as Schumacher suggested, the solution to environmental problems does not lie in greater scientific or technological expertise but in changing people's ideas and values.

Tokenism

Most Christians have a superficial understanding of environmental theology and ethics. Many would regard nature as essentially separate from themselves and from God.

Churches, like other institutions, find it easy to respond to environmental concern on a superficial level:

- An "environmental" sermon is preached by a church leader on the Feast of St Francis.
- A statement voicing "extreme concern" is issued on World Environment Day.
- At a local level, a special occasion such as Harvest is used to highlight the issue.

These are all better than nothing. But there is a danger that such an approach allows the environment to be treated as a "specialist" or minority concern, rather than of importance to every Christian. It thus marginalises the problem.

Rethinking

Our minds matter. And as Christians we need to think more deeply about the environment in particular.

- Sermons are based on theology, explicitly or otherwise. Most 20th century theology has centred on human beings rather than the whole creation. We need new theological insights through which to analyse and respond to the environmental challenge. The Church's teaching on the environment must be developed within an adequate intellectual framework.

- We cannot make sense of the natural world if we do not understand its Creator. Equally, our experience of life cannot be explained merely in terms of our relationship with God without reference to our relationship with the rest of His creation. The Church's teaching should enable Christians to make sense of the world around them, and needs also to offer a vision capable of galvanising people's energies to respond to the environmental crisis.

- ☛ More needs to be taught about the intimacy of the relationship between divinity and the material creation, God and the world. Only then will more Christians appreciate that God is continually active in creation.

- ☛ There is a need for effective communication at the level of ordinary churchgoers and in Sunday School lessons. Young children often arrive at misconceptions through weak and simplified teaching, such as the idea that God lives up in the sky, wholly separate from His creation. This kind of image can become deeply embedded in people's minds and imaginations.

Social ethics

Historically the Church has played a major part in shaping people's ethics. It is important that the whole of creation is embraced in such teaching. Most churches teach much more about personal ethics such as honesty and fidelity, than about social ethics such as justice and sustainability.

Christians do not have all the answers. The Church should not pretend that it is able to provide an infallible response to every environmental concern. Its teaching should, however, equip Christians to make the broader ethical decisions we face today with greater confidence.

St Egbert's Action Plan

1. We must rethink our theology
We will reconsider the theology which underlies our church's teaching ministry. We will read Christian books and articles on environmental issues. We will use sermons and study groups to explore and rethink our ideas.

2. We must encourage the young
Our children and young people are especially concerned about the environment. We will listen to them, and pay particular attention to their need to understand the Christian faith in the context of the world around them.

3. We must promote good stewardship
We will use the church magazine, newssheet and notice board to provide details of local recycling facilities, sources of organic food and other environment-related information. We will publish environmental "topical tips" on a regular basis.

4. We must remember the wider world
We will foster our contact with Christians overseas. Most of our missionaries are primarily concerned with evangelism, but some can offer first hand experience of global environmental problems. We will arrange meetings when they are back home on leave.

THE NECESSITY OF POLITICS

Politics to the Christian is a means of responding to the social concerns which the gospel brings into our lives, and ordering society in such a way as to encourage people to take the best moral decisions.

Christianity should touch every sphere of our lives, including politics. Yet many Christians are reluctant to engage in political activity. Even some who are concerned about the environment avoid politics and concentrate their efforts on modifying their personal lifestyles.

Politically neutral?

The early Christians struggled to resolve how to respond to the power of the State (Acts 5:29, Rom 13:1). And certainly Christianity's relationship with politics will never be easy.

Some Christians try to resolve the tension by staying out of politics and denying that they *are* political. This negative attitude to politics is often rooted in the dualism which separates the material and the spiritual. They may believe that a Christian's duty is exclusively to evangelise and that any attempt to transform the world is in vain.

It is of course our duty to worship God and to preach the gospel. But the gospel is the promise that the *whole* creation will be renewed. The Church cannot dismiss the Bible's teaching in the spheres of economics and social justice and elbow God out of these parts of life.

Indeed there is no such thing as political neutrality. The rejection of politics by Christians is a profoundly *political* act, because it represents an acceptance of the status quo, or at least a tolerance towards it.

Christians who try to adopt lifestyles consistent with their beliefs, soon discover obstacles which can only be removed through action by political authorities. The willingness of local authorities to take cycling seriously in road planning, determines how safe and convenient it is to use bicycles rather than cars. Adequate recycling facilities are necessary if people are to recycle waste rather than put it in dustbins. Local authorities have to finance the necessary investment, and often this depends in turn on central government.

Some politicians have suggested that the environment should not be a "party political" issue. They imply that there might be a consensus response. But the reality is that people have different interests in the environment (motorists and rail users, farmers and ramblers, and so forth) and politics is essentially about resolving the inevitable conflicts.

An effective response to environmental problems must therefore include a political element.

The Bible and politics

Biblical passages concerning peace, justice and reconciliation demand consideration of our own social organisation and government.

There are literally hundreds of Biblical texts calling for justice. More is said in the Bible about politics than about charismatic gifts or the return of Christ. Old Testament laws in Exodus, Leviticus and Deuteronomy to help the poor, marginalised and

"If we try to be passive or to ignore what is happening about us then we are merely saying that we accept the way things are as the way God wants them to be."

Paul Marshall, *Thine is the Kingdom*

suffering shaped the economy of the Israelite community.

These laws (on land redistribution and interest rates, for example) are often disregarded by Christians, dismissed as irrelevant to the contemporary world. Yet Jesus reiterated the message of hope for the poor proclaimed in the Jubilee laws (Luke 4:18 cf Lev 25:10), and the first Christian communities lived by the same principles (Acts 2:44- 45).

A political kingdom?

Although Christianity demands political engagement, no particular system or political agenda can be directly equated with God's kingdom. Christians can work within different political parties or campaign organisations to achieve similar goals. A diversity of opinion is inevitable, even among Christians, and indeed healthy.

There is widespread cynicism about politics and politicians. People are bored with meaningless slogans, suspicious of politicians' motives, confused by the lack of ideological clarity, and dislike the hypocrisy.

Such cynicism needs to be overcome through a more positive and honest approach to politics. For Christians this will be based on a vision of the prospect of a kingdom of peace, justice and environmental sustainability.

"The Scriptures speak to us continually, incessantly and unremittingly about justice and politics"

Paul Marshall, *Thine is the Kingdom*

Single-issue campaigns are common in politics. But an ecological perspective highlights the underlying connections between issues. There may be unexpected alliances: "Linking environmental issues with issues of disarmament is as necessary as linking disarmament and abortion. In all these issues we work from a foundation of belief in the sanctity of life" (Mary Jegen).

St Egbert's Action Plan

1. We must promote political activity

We will arrange a meeting to enable our church members to learn about connections between the Christian faith and different political ideologies. At the next election we will organise a forum for candidates to express their opinions on the issues of greatest interest to local Christians.

2. We must take local action

Our church has an interest in political decisions which affect our locality, especially those relating to the environment. We will increase our awareness of local planning developments, using the church magazine, newsletters and notice boards.

3. We must support campaigns

We will identify those campaigns on environmental or development issues which would be widely supported in our church. We will contact the relevant organisation and offer help. We will raise campaign funds through a local collection or event.

THINK!

The Green Party rejects secular humanism and its manifestos explicitly acknowledge the spiritual dimension to life.

Think of three reasons which may justify voting for the Green Party and three reasons for rejecting it and voting for one of the alternatives.

Is your answer based on reading all of the parties' manifestos, or merely from reports in the media?

AUDITING THE CHURCH

Ecology and economics share the same Greek root, *oikos*, "house" (or, more loosely, our dwelling place or world). And we all inhabit one "house": planet Earth.

How the church manages its affairs (its *economy*) should be influenced by its relationships with the outside world (its *ecology*).

Traidcraft was one of the first national organisations to have a social audit.

So what can local churches do to respond to the needs of this "outside world"?

Increasingly businesses and other organisations commission environmental audits in order to monitor the impact of their activities on the environment. These assess their performance by a broader measure than the financial balance sheet. Some go even further and have wider-ranging "social audits".

Such a practice could be carried out by local churches. It would help them discover how far they matched fine words with action. Here are some issues which could be included in an audit:

The church as consumer

Through our decisions as consumers we can have an influence on the economy: what is produced and by whom. Christians should be at the forefront of the trend towards "ethical consumption". Local churches can play a part:

Food and drink. Are refreshments served in church wholesome or simply the cheapest available? At functions at which meals are served, is meat from factory farmed animals avoided? Are vegetarian alternatives offered? Is organic produce used? Are disposable items such as cups, plates and cutlery avoided?

Paper. Is recycled stationery used? Is discarded paper recycled? Is photocopying always doubled sided? Is scrap paper used wherever appropriate? Is recycled kitchen roll and toilet paper used? Are stickers applied to reuse old envelopes?

Cleaning products. Are chlorine-based bleaches and phosphate-based detergents avoided?

Choosing ethical suppliers. Is attention paid to the ethical record of the manufacturer when products are purchased? Many churches have Traidcraft stalls, selling products from poorer countries which have been traded at a fair price.

Sharing together

Sharing is a form of bonding, an act of communion. The early Christians shared their possessions (Acts 4:32). Everything in the church belonged to the whole.

How do church members relate to each other in material terms? Is there a big gulf between the rich and the poor? Are opportunities created for people to share possessions, perhaps by operating a "tool bank", or through a notice board to enable the use of each others' possessions? Is car sharing encouraged?

Christians as investors

Most of us use a bank account, have some savings, are building up a pension, or are buying a house. Increasing people are using ethical criteria when they make investments – pensions, endowment policies, life assurance or other savings.

Where does your local church have its funds invested? Are ethical criteria used in determining where they are put? Have members of the congregation easy access to advice about ethical investment?

Church premises

Many churches have buildings which are architecturally impressive but consume a lot of energy. The cost of heating large, tall buildings for short periods of time is high. Also, churches are valuable buildings which, when not in use, represent a community facility which is being wasted.

Has your church considered ways of reducing its heating costs? Does it use low energy light bulbs wherever possible? When it purchases items such as furniture, are environmental factors considered? Is there space on the site to provide recycling facilities for local people? Could the church building be used more often?

Church land

At a national, regional and local level, churches own considerable amounts of land. Most local churches are responsible for some land – their grounds, a graveyard, or a vicarage garden. Some churches have planted a "Bible garden".

Is the soil fed with organic matter from a compost heap? Is the use of chemicals avoided? Is there an area set aside for wildlife? Could a scheme be established for church members to share an allotment?

The Church in the community

Churches have always been important to community life. They are also communities in themselves, bringing together people who share similar commitments, values and goals.

Does the church remain open and serve the local community throughout the week? Do members of the church monitor any plans to change the use of nearby land and facilities, assess the environmental impact, and respond if it is negative?

Travelling to church

A high proportion of car journeys are less than two miles: these include many people travelling to church.

Are cycle racks available outside your church, to encourage cycling and avoid the risk of bicycle theft? Is there a car sharing scheme to take people to church? Could car-owning church members who live near each other give up one car and share the other?

Worship

Our beliefs are reinforced by affirmations made in hymns, songs and liturgies. These need our attention. Contemporary song books contain many songs with lyrics about personal devotion and few that focus on our involvement in the world.

Have you studied the words used in your church's services to ensure that they reflect an appropriate theological stance? Do you choose hymns carefully, avoiding those rooted in a dualistic philosophy and negative towards the rest of creation? Have you carried out any symbolic acts which affirm the goodness of nature, such as planting trees, or decorating the church seasonally using locally sourced flowers and other materials?

Celebration

Celebrations are important points in the calendar when we remember past events, take note of seasonal change, or mark a special occasion. They are times for reflection, but also for joy and thanksgiving. A wide range of material for celebrating God's creation is now available, including liturgies, games for young people, posters and study material.

Does your church express its environmental awareness through seasonal celebrations at Lent, Easter, Rogation, Harvest, All Hallow's Eve, Advent and Christmas? And does it take steps to avoid the profligacy of these festivals, by minimising new purchases?

Community Wholefoods, one of Britain's largest suppliers of wholefoods, is run by Christians.

SOMETHING TO DO

Invite your local church to carry out an ecological audit, using the model in Christian Ecology Link's pack *Steps Towards Sustainability* (see page 86). Then reflect on people's response. Were they very receptive, interested, or dismissive?

If you got a rather cool reception, consider why this might be. What do you think you could do to help the situation, before making the suggestion again?

St Egbert's Action Plan

We must carry out an ecological audit

We will assess our roles as consumers and investors, collectively and individually, to ensure that we minimise our environmental impact. We will seek to reduce our energy use and make the best use of our land. We will ensure that our worship and celebrations are sensitive to environmental concerns.

GOING FURTHER

RESOURCES

Some of the material in this Unit is taken from Christian Ecology Link's sustainability pack (details on page 86).

A short video entitled *How Green is Your Church?* is available from Christian Ecology Link.

The *UK Evangelical Environmental Network* links Christians involved in environmental concerns at a professional level. Based at St Peter's Church, Vere Street, London W1M 9HP.

A Rocha – Christians in Conservation promotes Conservation Sunday. Based at 3 Hooper Street, Cambridge CB1 2NZ.

The *Church and Conservation Project* provides information on managing churchyards and encouraging wildlife. It is based at the Arthur Rank Centre, National Agricultural Centre, Stoneleigh, Warwicks CV8 2LZ.

A handbook *Wildlife in Church and Churchyard* by Nigel Cooper has been produced by the Council for the Care of Churches (Church House Publishing).

The Church of Scotland has produced two guides on energy saving measures for churches, *Make the Most of It* and *Make Even More of It* (121 George Street, Edinburgh EH2 4YN).

The *Christian Ethical Investors Group* is based at 90 Booker Avenue, Bradwell Common, Milton Keynes, MK13 8EF.

Most denomination headquarters and some aid and development organisations have produced resources for worship on an environmental theme. The *Iona Community Worship Book* is impressive (Wild Goose Publications, 840 Govan Road, Glasgow G51 3UU).

A daily *Prayer Guide for Care of Creation* is available from Philip Clarkson-Webb, 15 Valley View, Southborough, Tunbridge Wells, Kent TN4 0SY.

Barbara Wood has daily readings and prayers in *Our World, God's World: Reflections and Prayers for the Environment* (Bible Reading Fellowship).

The journal *Ecotheology* is available from the Sheffield Academic Press, 19 Kingfield Road, Sheffield S11 9AS.

The Church as ecosystem

How far can the church use concepts developed by ecologists? Perhaps it could view its own environment as a form of ecosystem. Churchgoers would be seen as communities of (human) organisms amidst the environment's living components (the local community, wildlife in the churchyard) and its non-living components (the pews, the organ, the church hall). Some interesting questions then arise.

Living together

How do these organisms live and function together? Are some dominant over others? Are relationships characterised by competition or co-operation? Do all of the members of the congregation adapt to a "niche", or do some feel out of place?

Is the ecosystem "complex", or are most churchgoers like-minded and from the same background? In the natural world diversity is often essential for stability. Is there enough diversity in your church or do its practices tend to be uniform? Does criticism that "all churches seem the same" have validity? Are its services varied enough? Is there a lack of spontaneity?

Change

All environments undergo a process of continual change ("ecological succession"). Sometimes the change from one definable stage to another is slow, while at other times it is dramatic.

Can an analogy be drawn with stages in church history, such as the Reformation, the 19th century evangelical revival, liberalism and modern orthodoxy? As each stage builds on the past, is our Christian understanding becoming more mature? Or perhaps there will be a succession of stages, culminating in a return to the primaeval state as original truths of Christianity are rediscovered?

Leadership and growth

Some people accept the need for change in the environment. Others prefer nature to remain unaffected by a human presence.

Are our Church leaders the equivalent of preservationists, disliking any change in their environment? Or are they like environmental managers, responding positively to change but seeking to ensure that it takes place in a positive fashion?

Can you identify an "environmental resistance" that prevents the church population from increasing exponentially?

Additional reading

On the church's environmental responsibility, see Mary Jegen and Larry Rasmussen in Wesley Granberg-Michaelson's *Tending the Garden*. The final chapter of Tim Cooper's *Green Christianity* is relevant. Ghillean Prance has edited a collection of essays about Christians caring for the environment overseas, *Missionary Earthkeepers*. Sean McDonagh has written *Passion for the Earth* on the WCC theme of "Justice, Peace and the Integrity of Creation", as has David Gosling in *A New Earth*.

"Ecology provides a framework for perceiving the church's life and relationship to creation, rather than merely presenting a set of external issues to be confronted."

Wesley Granberg-Michaelson, *A Worldly Spirituality*

REGISTERING FOR TUTOR SUPPORT?

If you would like the help and support of a tutor, please fill in the form below. We will put you in touch with your tutor as soon as possible. You may photocopy this form if you prefer.

I want to study **Sustaining the Earth** with a tutor. Please register my name.

Name	
Address	
Postcode	Telephone

I enclose a cheque for £50.00 to cover the cost of tuition.

Please use the space below to tell us about yourself: something about your background and why you are interested in doing this course. It will be useful to your tutor to have this information.

Send this form, with your remittance, to: St John's Extension Studies, Bramcote, Nottingham NG9 3RL. Telephone 0115 925 1117 for enquiries and credit card payments. You can fax this form on 0115 943 6438.